Overcoming the Rating Game

	DATE		

Also by Paul A. Hauck

How to Get the Most Out of Life
The Three Faces of Love
Overcoming Jealousy and Possessiveness
Brief Counseling with RET
How to Stand Up for Yourself
Marriage Is a Loving Business
How to Do What You Want to Do:
The Art of Self-Discipline
Overcoming Worry and Fear
Overcoming Frustration and Anger
Overcoming Depression

Overcoming the Rating Game

Beyond Self-Love—Beyond Self-Esteem

Paul A. Hauck

Westminster/John Knox Press
Louisville, Kentucky

First published in Great Britain in 1991
by Sheldon Press, SPCK, Holy Trinity Church,
Marylebone Road, London NW1 4DU

First American edition

Published by Westminster/John Knox Press
Louisville, Kentucky

This book is printed on acid-free paper that meets
the American National Standards Institute Z39.48 standard. ∞

Library of Congress Cataloging-in-Publication Data

Hauck, Paul A.
   Overcoming the rating game : beyond self-love—beyond self-esteem / Paul A. Hauck. — 1st American ed.
       p.   cm.
   ISBN 0-664-25310-5 (alk. paper)

   1. Self-acceptance.   2. Self-evaluation.   3. Inferiority complex.   4. Rational-emotive psychotherapy.   I. Title.
BF575.S37H38 1991
158'.1—dc20   91-40524

To my loyal secretaries, Kathy Holladay and
Nanci Perkins, for their patience and good humour
during the many changes this manuscript went through.

Contents

Foreword

I have wrestled with the problem of self-worth ever since I originated rational-emotive therapy (RET) in 1955 and started to practise it with a large number of clients. RET is one of the most philosophical of therapies and directly deals with people's main cognitive and emotional problems, particularly with the question of their worth to themselves and to other humans. After much thought and clinical practice, I came up with several unique solutions to the question of how people had best rate – or *not* rate – themselves; and, in trying these out with many clients, readers and workshop participants, I found them to be much more effective than when I previously practised psychoanalytic therapy.

Although the RET position on psychotherapy and self-evaluation has now been adopted by large numbers of rational-emotive and cognitive-behavioural therapists, and although hundreds of articles and books favouring this position have been published to date, no writer has described RET theory and practice as clearly as Paul Hauck. Beginning in 1967 with *The Rational Management of Children* (published in the UK by Sheldon as *How to Bring up your Child Successfully*), and continuing in the 1970s and 1980s with well-written self-help books on overcoming depression, worry and fear, frustration and anger, jealousy and possessiveness, and other common emotional problems, Paul's writings have helped, I can safely say, an enormous number of people who have used them as self-help materials; and they have also been used by many therapists to hasten the recovery of their clients. Our therapists at the Institute for Rational-Emotive Therapy in New York have routinely recommended them to clients at our psychological clinic and they report considerable success with them. The Institute also regularly sells thousands of Paul's books through a biannual catalogue of RET materials.

Paul Hauck's previous books have often touched on the central question of human worth, but in the present volume he

1

considers it in much more detail. He gives many reasons why people cannot legitimately be given global or personhood ratings, although it is quite important that they evaluate the effectiveness of their own traits and performances. He shows, as I have 'shockingly' said in my writings and workshops, that when we strive for 'self-esteem' we often make ourselves sick rather than healthy, ineffective rather than efficient. Why? Because 'self-esteem' usually depends on our performing well and being approved by significant others; and who among us consistently measures up – yes, *measures* up – in these respects?

Paul also ties up self-acceptance with tolerance for others and with self-discipline – two other key traits that RET helps people to achieve. In a book of this small size he comes up with a remarkably large number of profound self-help ideas.

Let me restate some of the best RET philosophies about self-evaluation by paraphrasing a statement on human worth that I have frequently made to my clients and at public lectures, as well as in some of my own writings – particularly *Reason and Emotion in Psychotherapy*, *Humanistic Psychotherapy: The Rational-Emotive Approach*, and *How to Stubbornly Refuse to Make Yourself Miserable About Anything – Yes, Anything!*

'As a person, you were born and reared with two strong tendencies: to rate or evaluate your acts, thoughts, feelings, and behaviours, to determine whether they are "good" or "effective"; and to rate or measure your "self", your "being", your "essence", your "totality". In RET, we encourage you to continue the first of these – performance ratings – but to be most cautious about the second – self-ratings.

'Although self-ratings seem "naturally" and "automatically" to stem from measuring your deeds, they mainly do so because you arbitrarily *define* your estimation of your self in terms of how you measure (some of) your traits. The two are not *actually* related because, if you want to evaluate your "self" or "essence" at all (which you really *don't* have to do), you can measure it in terms of almost anything: for example, in relation to your aliveness, your upbringing, your nationality, your height, your appetite, your religion, your home, or almost anything else. Moreover, the weights that you give to these measures of your worth can also easily be arbitrary. Thus, you can say "I am a good person because I am short" or "I am a good person because I am tall". Or you can say "I am a worthy individual because people like me" or "I am a worthy individual because only a few select people like me".

'If you define your self-worth in terms of almost any specific criterion, especially "good" performances, you are likely to create emotional trouble. When, for one reason or another, you do not have "good" deeds to your credit, you are a worthless person; and when you do have them, you almost inevitably worry about not having them *later*. So you can't win!

'After giving much thought to the problem of self-evaluation, RET has come up with two fairly good – though still imperfect – solutions. The first is difficult but still tenable: decide not to rate your "self", your "being", your "essence", *at all*. If you want to assume that you have a "self" or an "essence", OK – even though you will have some difficulty, as scholars have had for ages, in accurately defining it. Anyway, stubbornly refuse to rate, measure, or evaluate it. Only – yes, *only* – rate what you *do* (so that you can discover how to do better and to enjoy yourself more) – and not what you *are*. If you want to label yourself as "you", then acknowledge that *you* are responsible for what you do, and that you *act* irresponsibly when you do poorly (e.g., lie to yourself or others). But still don't rate your *youness* or *self*. *Only* rate your irresponsible (as well as your good) *behaviour*.

'This is probably the most elegant RET solution to the problem of self-worth and will get you into practically no trouble. As a less elegant but still viable option, you can rate your *self* or *being*, but only in terms of some general, safe concept, which is never likely to change, at least during your lifetime, or can only change by your deciding to change it. Thus, you can say "I am a good person because I exist or am alive". You then can't be "bad" or "no good" until you are dead. Or you can say "I am good because I am a fallible, imperfect human" – and then you can be pretty sure that this will, as long as you live, always be true! Or you can say "I am good because God loves me" and you can then decide that God exists and always loves you.

'Either of these solutions to the problem of self-worth will work. Take your choice. For rating your "self" is a *choice*, not a *necessity*. You can choose to rate or not to rate your "self", as long as you (for practical purposes) rate your (and others') performances. And if you choose to be a "good" person, you can strongly convince yourself that you are good because you choose to see yourself as good; and you choose to see yourself as good *whether or not* you perform well and *whether or not* others approve of you. Having *decided* this, you can then ask yourself how you can more effectively continue to live, to enjoy yourself, and to contribute to the social milieu in which you *choose* to live.'

If you want some excellent arguments to support these views, you will find them in abundance in Paul Hauck's very readable book.

Albert Ellis, PhD, President
Institute for Rational-Emotive Therapy
45 East 65th Street
New York, NY 10021, USA

Introduction

This is my fourteenth book on the subject of self-help psychology based on the principles of cognitive-behavioural therapy with particular emphasis on the best variety of that type of therapy called rational-emotive therapy (RET). The subjects covered in my past works have been the common emotional disturbances: depression, anger, fear, jealousy and excessive passivity. I have also shown how RET applies to the rearing of children, to love and marriage, and to assertiveness.

These volumes constitute a wealth of information on those psychological facts which practically all of us need to live harmoniously our everyday lives. They have been a labour of love spread over the past twenty-five years. I have been told that there is some repetition of material from one book to the next. I agree. But that is unavoidable. What I have done is to show how the principles of RET and cognitive-behavioural therapy apply to specific emotional conditions. When I wrote about self-discipline I called upon some principles of RET which I had also used to describe excessive passivity. And that is how I have progressed from book to book, always focusing on a new subject but always within the framework of RET.

For many months after my last book I felt I had said all I ever wanted to say about common emotional disorders. However, it slowly began to dawn on me that another volume was called for, one which was of great importance and which had not been written before for the layman by any cognitive-behaviourist I knew of.

This is that book. It addresses the extremely important subject of the inferiority complex and how it is shaped. Now that I am immersed in the subject, I wonder why I waited until now to write it. Perhaps I have unconsciously kept the most important for the last.

As usual, before I began this book I had only an incomplete idea of how RET explains low self-esteem. Once I began the outline and the writing, the pieces began to fall nicely into place and I am now convinced after many clinical observations, and a few chats with Dr Albert Ellis, that my thoughts about inferiority feelings are basically correct.

That makes me feel very content. It's like tying a ribbon around a Christmas present.

1

How to Recognize
Low Self-esteem

I realized many years ago what self-hate is capable of doing to
a human being. I was the chief psychologist at a state hospital
for the mentally ill and was conversing with a gentleman, well
into his thirties, who told me how he felt about himself: he was
a despicable human being, there was nothing particularly
worthwhile about him, anyone who ever got close enough to
know him intimately would sooner or later realize that he was
a totally inferior human being, and that there was something
in his body which was black and slimy and had an awful odour.

I was stunned at the severity of his negative judgments. The
fellow was actually a very pleasant person, pleasing in his
appearance, inoffensive in his behaviour, and yet he made
these statements with the utmost sincerity. It took me some
time to realize that he really did believe all these cruel things
he was saying about himself.

Sometime thereafter I was watching a beauty contest on
television. There were contestants from all around the world.
These lovely young ladies were asked the question: 'Who
would you like to be if you could be anyone you chose?' Some
of the contestants gave the names of famous women such as
movie stars, wives of famous men, or rich women. Two
contestants, however, both from South America, answered
the question differently. Without a moment's hesitation they
said they would like to be themselves.

There you have the difference between an unhealthy and a
healthy self-image: one hated himself, the others accepted
themselves. The one was highly disturbed, the others very
content. One was suicidal, the others full of life.

That simple difference – how they rated themselves – made
all the difference between these people.

In the years since those two observations took place I have
come to have an even greater appreciation for the effects of

our self-perceptions on our lives and futures. I am convinced that what others think of us is not as important as what we think of ourselves. If we hate ourselves we will surely suffer for it and will carry a living hell inside us which will affect us for an entire lifetime. Correspondingly, if we are gentle with ourselves and view ourselves as acceptable people who can be forgiven our errors and weaknesses, we can go through life in a condition of calmness and relative happiness.

The purpose of this book is to teach you how to achieve attitudes about yourself that you will *want* to live with. In the following pages you will be introduced to ideas which are so simple and yet so powerful that they can change your life. I will be showing you several techniques you can follow which will carry you over the hurdles which life will put in your way and which will allow you to be in touch with the potential you have for personal fulfilment.

As simple as these techniques will seem, that is also how difficult they will be to put into practice. You will need to develop psychological skills in just the same way as you have to exercise in order to remain in good health. You cannot read this book through once and rise from your chair a changed person. To change, you will have to think hard and long about the philosophies which have given you feelings of inferiority and guilt all of your life. You may accomplish peace of mind in a matter of months. But it is more likely that you will require periodic applications of these principles over the next several years of your life and only then will you begin to notice how you are changing and feeling better.

Do not be put off by the fact that this will be time-consuming and require discipline. The goal you are seeking is well worth the effort no matter how exhausting or how long you struggle to change your self-ratings. Even if you are only partially successful, you will still be well rewarded for whatever gains you have made. The person who wants to lose a hundred pounds in weight knows full well that with constant effort the task may take a hundred weeks. But even if no more than fifty pounds are shed, that is still an appreciable loss and it makes the effort well worth while.

So do not lose heart, realize that this is a problem which

practically everyone in the whole world has, and that if others can do it so can you. You may not do it as well as others, you may not do it as quickly as others, but that doesn't matter. The important point is that you can get better at reducing your feelings of inferiority and can learn to be gentler with yourself. If you can learn to be a self-hating and inferior-feeling person you can also learn to be a self-accepting person and refuse to think badly about yourself. People can change and have proved they can change. What you were at one time in your life you do not have to be tomorrow. The only reason you are continuing to behave in a self-defeating way today is that you have been practising negative thinking for years. That is unnecessary, it is unhealthy, and it is nothing more than a bad habit. If you think of most of your emotional problems as only bad habits you will get a good idea of what your task is all about. All of your life you have changed your habits as you needed to. I am now asking that you change several more because they are crucial to your happiness and your emotional well-being. Habits are learned, and habits can be unlearned.

Join me now in this journey of exploration as we study this extremely important human desire not to be our own worst enemy.

The signs of a poor self-image

Feelings of inferiority

It is usually quite easy to detect people who have a low regard for themselves. The most obvious sign is that they feel inferior to others. This can be seen in the simple act of shaking hands. I very seldom come across people with a weak handshake who have a lot of social confidence. The two simply don't seem to go together. And if the person looks away while being introduced, or ordinarily shows poor eye contact, you can be reasonably sure that this is another indication of personal rejection. Why else would the person avoid looking into your eyes? When I have explored this subject with my own clients the reason for avoiding eye contact seems to be that they are afraid that we will look inside them and see all their faults and weaknesses. Either that, or they do not want to see what they are convinced will happen: others will show their disapproval through disinterest, teasing or airs of superiority. However, if you think well of yourself, and refuse to believe you are evil or worthless, then why in heaven's name wouldn't you look people straight in the eye? Obviously you wouldn't have anything to be afraid of. You'd feel every bit as good as they think they are and there would be nothing to hide. You would enter the conversation with a feeling of curiosity and pleasure, wondering who this person is that you are talking to and whether this isn't a potential friend or, at the very least, an interesting and pleasant brief encounter.

Frequent apologies

The second common characteristic we see in people who feel inferior is that they often apologize. They are always asking to be forgiven or to be excused for minor errors of judgment or etiquette. They are so conscious of doing things badly and so brainwashed into thinking that everybody is going to object to what they think or do that they apologize even before they say or do something.

This practice of apologizing can often be seen when people make comparisons. The hostess who says to her dinner guests 'This roast isn't as good as I usually serve' is jumping the gun and predicting her meal is going to be thought poorly of. In this way she deals with any objection before it arises.

People who repeatedly preface their remarks with 'I'm probably wrong, but . . .' are again expressing the same sense of insecurity about what they are going to say. However, they are beating their critics to the punch by admitting beforehand that they might be wrong.

Apologies are, of course, a perfectly proper means of dealing in society with errors in behaviour. When carried to the extreme, however, they become annoying and bothersome and are very clear signals that the person doing the apologizing anticipates constant and repeated rejection. It is much more genuine, if you have done something wrong, to apologize for it sincerely and briefly and then drop the subject. Wanting to be excused and forgiven for every little mistake simply turns people off because they can see that they are dealing with a very scared and insecure person.

Fear of failure

If you are afraid to try new things because you won't do well and will cause people to laugh, you're advertising your inferiority feelings just as clearly as if you had on a T-shirt with the words 'I hate myself' splashed across your chest.

As you will see in the following pages, fear of failure is generally associated with a low self-image. However, what most people regard as failure, people who are mentally in good health regard as merely mistakes from which they can learn. They are not terribly uncomfortable with them, in fact they often welcome the opportunity to try something, knowing full well that they will do badly at it. But they view mistakes as stepping stones to success. In this way they learn what not to do, realizing that they wouldn't know if they didn't try at least to find out.

Conformity

People who feel inferior also show their insecurity in the way they brag about their possessions, their clothes, their cars, and the people they know. The high-school youngster who wouldn't be seen dead in school with an article of clothing that didn't carry a designer label is simply advertising his inferiority to the whole world. He is saying that unless he has fashionable clothes he obviously is worthless and deserves to feel humiliated. Rubbish. How can you be a superior person because you put on one pair of jeans rather than another? Or how can you become a better human being because you wear an expensive suit rather than a cheap one? How can you look down on others because you know the president of the bank or the leaders of the community? Such things have nothing whatever to do with your personal worthwhileness. Yet we usually judge ourselves by these things.

This tendency to rate ourselves by whom we know, by what we wear and by how much money we make is such a strong one, and has been with us for so many thousands of years that it will not change overnight. But let that be somebody else's mistake. Don't put yourself down because you don't wear the latest fashion, or you didn't go to the right school, or you don't vacation at the swankiest resort. There is obviously nothing wrong with being able to live well but that only has to do with luxury and fun, not superiority. If you want to flash your diamond rings, your Rolex watch, or your Gucci shoes, more power to you. But don't think this somehow makes you better than others. It only makes you richer. There is nothing wrong with being rich. Good for you again. But it doesn't make you better as a *human being* than somebody who doesn't have that much money. It means you have succeeded in acquiring more wealth, that and nothing more.

Guilt

When you say that you *feel* guilty you are telling yourself that you have not only done something wrong, but that you are also *evil* for doing so. That will usually have a very bad effect upon you. How could it be otherwise?

In one of the following chapters I will go into considerable detail about why you should never *feel* guilty, although it makes perfectly good sense for you to admit that you *are* guilty about any number of things.

Shyness

This is another very powerful indication that a person suffers from insecurity. The more fears you have the more you are admitting to yourself and to others that you don't have the confidence to handle a particular situation. And that, of course, usually leads to your believing that you are weak and deficient and you'll probably blame yourself for those short-comings.

Being filled with fear is the opposite of being filled with confidence. When you act in a confident manner you usually feel good about yourself, you feel secure, and you think you can take on the world. But, if you are afraid of giving a speech, or getting out on the dance floor or entering a room full of strangers, then clearly what you're saying to everybody is 'I'm afraid you are not going to like me because I don't know what to say. Maybe I'll make a fool of myself. What do you want to talk to me for anyway?' These are a few of the classical put-downs common to fearful people.

Fault-finding

Another category of people who are insecure, even though it doesn't look that way to most people at first blush, are those who constantly find fault with others. The father who repeatedly puts his son down by telling him he is no good, is in all likelihood prompted to behave in this unkind way because he's threatened by the boy. I have seen a number of children who were perfectly fine youngsters, good looking, bright, and reasonably obedient, who simply could not please their parents. In some cases the parents were so insecure about their own worthwhileness that they were jealous of the popularity their own growing children achieved.

Such mothers and fathers may look for all the world as though they are strong and tough, but under the surface they are scared that a little infant coming into the family is going to take their partner from them. Or that their growing sons or daughters will be handsome and successful people who will marry well and do better in life than they did. As a result they try in unconscious ways (or perhaps even in semi-conscious ways) to sabotage success in their children. That is a pathetic situation but I'm afraid it happens all too often.

Defensiveness

Getting defensive when criticized is another major sign that you are suffering from inferiority. Yet being criticized is hardly a serious happening, unless, of course, you think that being found fault with is a disgraceful and shameful act. To think that, however, you would have to be quite convinced that some of the accusations being made of you are in fact true and that, if true, would prove you are a failure as a human being.

Stop and think. If you had a healthy feeling about yourself it would not occur to you to get painfully sensitive about being found fault with, you would not be afraid that perhaps what someone is telling you might be true. The secure person accepts the possibility that the criticism may in fact be accurate. If so, why not appreciate the advice? The best way to handle criticism is simply to ask yourself whether the comments being made about you are correct or not. If they are correct, what are you getting upset about? Why aren't you pleased that somebody is trying to help you understand one of your faults? Are you suggesting you shouldn't have faults? That would surely be absurd, wouldn't it? And, when you have a fault and you don't know it, isn't someone doing you a big favour by telling you so? For example, suppose you have body odour but are unaware of it, wouldn't you be grateful somebody told you? And if the comment were not true, again there is no reason to become defensive and upset since all you have to do is grant others the right to their opinions (wrong as they might be). After all, two people have a perfect right to disagree. If you do this – agree to disagree – then there is again really no reason to get upset over a criticism.

Those people who insist they have to defend their honour if they are called vulgar names are also showing their insecurity. A name does not turn you into whatever the name describes. If someone calls you a dumb ox, that hardly makes you one. That is nothing to get upset about. The other person has a perfect right to think about you as he or she wishes. You have the same right, too. And if the person wants to make it publicly known that he or she thinks this way about you, again, tolerate this as a simple difference of opinion. To get into a fist fight, or to endanger your life or safety because someone called you a name is really a foolish exercise in macho defensiveness.

Relax. You either are or you are not what you are called. If you are, accept it in good grace and change if you possibly can. If you aren't what you're accused of, ignore it, consider the other person mistaken and go about your business. If you can do that you will demonstrate great strength, great control, and will be viewed by others as a stable person.

Possessiveness and Jealousy

Possessiveness and jealousy are typical emotions which again reveal insecurity and feelings of inferiority. What else would these two emotions signify? Possessiveness clearly reveals your insecurity simply by the fact that you think you can't live without a certain person and that you must have his or her constant attention. The degree to which you are threatened by your friend or partner showing interest in others is a direct measure of the degree to which you are unsure of yourself. It goes without saying that if you are not neurotically and obsessively concerned about the attentions and approval of the people in your life, you must think that you have enough strength and stability not to be disturbed by these lapses of attention. If you had more self-acceptance, it would simply not occur to you to be possessive!

And the same can be said for jealousy. You are jealous of others simply because you don't think you are worthy enough to hold on to their affections. If your partner spends time with someone else or seems to enjoy someone else's company, and you feel threatened, what else are you thinking except that you are afraid you will lose your partner to that person? And the more you act that way the more you must be saying that you are inferior and undesirable. Isn't that absurd?

Fear of rejection

People who accept themselves do not hesitate to disagree with public opinion. They know they will receive some rejection, but because they accept themselves so well, they are not destroyed if others dislike them. They understand very clearly that rejection is not *emotionally* painful unless they *make* it so. Only they can make it a painful experience. They do that by believing that being rejected proves they are awful and worthless persons and that the only way they can be respectable human beings is to be loved by certain people who are very important to them.

Why should you put the value you have for yourself in the hands of other people? Who are they to make these kinds of judgments about you? It is true that if you want to be approved of you will have to go along with people to *some* extent. But that doesn't mean that if you don't go along with them, and they don't like or accept you, you somehow are less of a human being. It simply means that you don't fit into that group and you had better find other people who like the kind of person you are.

Handling rejection from loved ones is admittedly a difficult task and requires lots of practice to cope with. But when you are able to do this you will feel stronger because you will have a degree of inner comfort which is not dependent upon the approval of every Tom, Dick and Harry.

Rejecting compliments

It should come as no surprise that complimenting people who think very badly about themselves simply does not work. They're not inclined to believe you if you do have decent things to say about them because they cannot believe anything flattering about themselves. Being able to receive a compliment means that you at least consider the possibility that somebody truly thinks well of you. But if you have been convicted of a crime, rejected by your parents, or failed to achieve what others were able to achieve, then it makes sense that a compliment is not going to ring true.

We tend to believe those statements about us which seem plausible. If someone describes you as the greatest dancer in the whole world you know they are pulling your leg. But if someone says that you are a good dancer and that you are easy to follow, that is a much more plausible statement. But if you tell a woman she is beautiful, but she thinks she is hideous, your compliment will fall on deaf ears. The next time you give compliments and you see the other person squirm at such remarks you can believe that he or she is very definitely trying to resolve an inconsistency: 'How can I be thought of so well when I feel I'm so bad?' The only way to resolve that puzzle is to conclude that the other person is simply being polite and would not make those remarks if he or she really knew you.

Even if you feel better after somebody has complimented you and your sense of pride has been strengthened, it unfortunately does not usually last. Unless you feel you are a decent and acceptable person, nothing anyone else can say will bring about lasting changes in you. It is what you believe about yourself that makes the big difference, not what others believe. It doesn't matter whether you believe that God is all-forgiving and all-loving, that your parents adore you, or that your children love you; none of this matters unless you feel you are an acceptable person and can straightforwardly, without shame or embarrassment, agree that some of the flattering things being said about you are in fact true.

Tolerance of deviant behaviour

We have all known people who have an incredible tolerance for sick and abusive behaviour. People who endure insults and criticism (to say nothing of physical abuse) obviously think very poorly of themselves. In some instances this is not true, as when a wife stays in an unhappy marriage because she needs her mate's financial support. I have known such women to endure abusive and deviant behaviour for years with the full intention of getting out of a bad marriage as soon as the last child left home.

Leaving such exceptions aside, however, those who yield to the will of highly disturbed people and put up with incredible physical and mental torture are clearly themselves quite disturbed. They have a deep need to suffer and tragically use their violent mates as means of proving on a daily basis just how undeserving they are. The longer such behaviour continues the more they hate themselves and the more they tolerate abusive behaviour from their disturbed partners.

Fear of competition

A contest always ends up with a winner and a loser. That is the nature of a contest. Therefore if you are one of those people who can't compete for fear you will do badly, you must have an inferiority complex. What else would it mean? If you can't get into a game and risk losing, you must think that your whole value as a human being is at stake. Or, if you can't enjoy performing for others and risk being evaluated, again, you have too little self-acceptance to protect you in the event that things go badly.

This is why some people shy away from introducing themselves to others. What if they were rejected? This is why some people will not give talks in public. Others will not raise their hands or stand up at a meeting to voice their opinions.

And others will not play a game of chess, go to a party, or do almost anything where they might be compared in some way with others. Are their clothes equal to those around them? Do they know enough about a subject to speak up? Will they be thought stupid because they are uninformed?

This fear of being thought badly of is so penetrating that millions of people throughout the world deny themselves opportunities for interesting experiences and a great deal of pleasure simply because they can't stand the competition which might show them up.

These people take life too seriously. They need to learn to loosen up, to relax, to enjoy an activity without thinking of it always as being a reflection of themselves. Why can't we run a race or make a comment and not have to be the best, the greatest, or the most beautiful?

Always being the best tends to be a crashing bore and never makes you much fun to be with. But worst of all, it is telling the world that you really feel terribly inferior if you can't stand the idea of coming in second or third or one-hundredth in comparison to others. People who think they *have* to be number one, actually think they are losers.

Do not be misled into believing that every emotional disturbance indicates inferiority. It is perfectly possible to have a superiority complex and be chronically upset. Angry people are sometimes troubled by inferiority, but often they are not. In fact they can become angry simply because they think they are so much better than others.

People who become depressed because they feel sorry for themselves or others again are not necessarily upset because of feeling inferior. These emotions come either from caring too much for others, or because we think the world owes us a living. This often has nothing to do with feelings of inferiority.

In the following pages you will learn how not to feel inferior or guilty. If this should be insufficient to handle some of your problems, I would urge you to read books on emotional control. Should you want to make personal contact with me I will provide you with my address and phone number at the end of this book.

This chapter has provided a fairly complete run-down of the signs of insecurity and inferiority. Don't be surprised if you have seen yourself described under some of these headings. You are, after all, a human being and you must have some faults. A few of those I've mentioned above probably describe you pretty well. If so, read this book carefully. You need to know how to cope with these problems. It will be hard work, but getting rid of inferiority should be the number one priority in your life. Until you can achieve this, anything else you attempt to do for your well-being, and for those around you, will be just that much harder.

2

How Bad Is This Problem?

When you boil it all down to its essentials, there are probably two reasons why people become psychologically disturbed. The first is that they make mountains out of molehills. The second is that they have low opinions of themselves. Sometimes these two problems go hand in hand, but they can also occur quite separately. For example, if a young fellow discovers, while driving home at night, that he is low on petrol and may have to walk ten miles to get home, he might be disturbed by the belief that having to walk ten miles at night is a potentially terrible and dangerous experience. This doesn't mean that he must also have a low opinion of himself. An inferiority feeling is not an automatic outcome of his wondering whether or not he is in serious trouble.

Now let's suppose this fellow is an actor and must perform in a play. He is very worried about how well he will do. Once again he can make a mountain out of a molehill and tell himself that it would be terrible not to do well because it could put him out of work. But at the same time he could also tell himself that such an experience would make him worthless, inferior, and a first-class loser who never succeeds at anything. Do you notice the harsh treatment he begins to subject himself to over the fact that he may not perform well? In this case the disturbance and the inferiority feelings go together.

Magnifying things out of proportion is an extremely common technique which people use to create disturbances. However, disapproving of yourself because your performance is inferior is also an extremely common human tendency. Everybody in the world makes both of these mistakes from time to time.

The tendency to feel inferior and unworthy is possibly strongest during the adolescent years when the ability to think rationally is less well developed. As we get older it gets easier for us to talk ourselves out of thinking that every frustration we have is the end of the world and it also gets easier for us not

20

to feel badly about ourselves when we do badly. Still, for most of the people over the entire face of this earth, the most common tendency in dealing with frustrations is to catastrophize over them on the one hand, and to put themselves down on the other hand. The problem is immense. It is universal.

Making yourself feel inferior is so serious it affects everything you do. Anything you manage to do after you blame yourself could practically always be done much more easily and better if you hadn't rejected yourself. When you get to the point where you can't stand yourself you begin to create a great many other problems in your life. A person who does one thing wrong and hates himself for it usually does another thing wrong. This circular process can go on and on until we punish ourselves more and more severely for our mistakes, which causes us to perform in increasingly negative ways, which leads us to punish ourselves again. It's a vicious circle.

An inferiority feeling does not go away on its own. It can be with you always, if you allow it. You may be content with your appearance one day, and the next day a more attractive person comes upon the scene. Then your inferiority feelings may act up again. If you feel worthless you will fail to speak up where your best interests are involved. You will hang out with friends who won't do you much good because you won't think you could attract more desirable friends. You will probably marry someone unsuitable for you because you wouldn't have the confidence to pursue someone more compatible. People with inferiority feelings associate with people with inferiority feelings. Negative self-ratings have extremely widespread effects. They will determine whether you ask for raises, the kind of job you get, whether you will be taking orders or giving orders, whether you let people cut in front of you in a movie line, and whether you will be popular or unpopular.

Rating yourself determines how you will deal with all the people you meet throughout your life and how you will deal with the good or bad fortune that comes your way. Individuals who don't rate themselves will take compliments gracefully and without embarrassment. People who rate themselves negatively always have trouble accepting compliments. They feel they are undeserved. They wonder if they haven't tricked other people into thinking they were intelligent or creative. In fact, there are many people who regard themselves as impostors and feel they are pulling the wool over everyone's eyes when they are told that they are brilliant or very talented. These people may have written a number of books or hold high university positions, or have invested wisely on the stock market to the point where they are very wealthy. Yet when they are complimented for their achievements they feel they are undeserving of such words of praise. They honestly believe they have deceived everyone and that if others knew them more intimately they would see how absolutely unworthy and inferior they actually are. It is difficult to realize how these people who have demonstrated superior performance in very difficult areas of achievement still think they have only done those things by luck and never because of their own natural talents and gifts. This condition has been called the *impostor complex.*

In short, if we believe that we are decent people we will let decent things happen to us. If we think we are unacceptable people we will see to it that unacceptable things happen.

Your self-rating is like a compass that guides you through a foggy night. Unless you know who you are and what you think of yourself, every other important interaction that you will have will be negatively affected by that ignorance. If you do not rate yourself your life will take one direction. If you do, your life takes an entirely different direction.

How bad is the problem? Pretty bad, not only in terms of how frequently it occurs, but also in terms of the damage it does to each and everyone of us if we fail to accept ourselves.

The religious question

Some of the most self-loathing people I have ever come across are those who claim to be the most religious. I have always been struck by this inconsistency. It has always been my conviction that those who truly follow the teachings of a religion will not feel wicked or unworthy. If such an emotion does exist in loyal followers of today's major faiths I believe that an enormous breach has opened up between what their churches teach them and what they *think* they teach them.

The problem of the inferiority complex is not only a religious matter but also a psychological one. As a psychologist I know something about how people develop self-ratings. Later I will address in considerable detail how good and moral people perform psychological acts of violence against themselves, why this had better stop and how it can be made to stop. Let's start by remembering Psalms 118:24: 'This is the day which the Lord hath made; we will rejoice and be glad in it.'

To do that, you must first of all have the positive self-acceptance which would permit you to rejoice and be glad.

The worst scenario

The familiar signs such as shyness, feelings of inferiority, unwarranted guilt feelings, inability to accept compliments, and jealousy are known to us all. What is not so evident to most people is that if these conditions persist over many years the self-esteem continues to deteriorate to a point where serious psychological conditions result. Before I describe them, let it be clearly understood that these conditions sometimes cause inferiority feelings, and sometimes they are the result of them. Either way, if you want to enjoy life you certainly want to do something about avoiding negative self-rating. Even more importantly, if you don't want to be absolutely miserable about life and struggle through it for all the years that you are on this earth, you certainly don't want to develop any of the following psychiatric conditions which often lead to constant discomfort, insecurity, and difficulty in your interpersonal relationships.

Dependent personality disorder

This condition is not as serious as the four which follow, but it is certainly disruptive enough in people's lives that it cannot be ignored and it comes essentially from the same tendency for people to rate themselves negatively; to distrust their abilities so that they do not develop performance-confidence; and to fail to get respect from others.

Dependent personalities seek to get through life by leaning on the strengths and the abilities of others rather than on their own. They are unable to make decisions unless great certainty exists that these decisions will be correct. One way to avoid this supposed horror would be to allow other people to make decisions for them. By doing this the persons on whom the dependent personality relies become stronger and more skilled at making decisions while dependent persons become weaker and weaker.

If you are very unsure of yourself you are likely to say you agree with people who argue with you even though you may believe they are wrong. You suspect that if you stand up for your viewpoint, you will be rejected, and, of course, that is unthinkable. Therefore, you agree to things you don't actually believe. But, being dependent, you have very little choice in the matter.

Dependent people do not initiate activities on their own, they wait for others to do so. They do not suggest which theatre to go to, where to holiday, which colour to paint a room, and so forth. It is always so much easier to let others make these decisions. Then they can't be accused later of having made a mistake.

Some of these people will do favours for others to the point where they are shamefully taken advantage of. A client of mine agreed to meet his cousin to help him repair his car. He was left waiting without an explanation. Yet he willingly went through that same experience several more times until finally the cousin actually did keep the appointment.

Dependent people are in such dire need of the approval of others that they dread being alone. Their degree of fear is directly correlated to how dependent they are. Therefore, when a relationship ends for these people, the consequences for them are a great deal more devastating than they are for people who are not so dependent. It follows, doesn't it, that the more you need people the more it hurts when you don't have their help.

Another outcome of that problem is the great fear you have of not just ending a relationship or losing a friend, but literally being abandoned. This is one of the reasons why men and women who are perfectly capable of living alone and not tolerating abusive behaviour, do so to extreme degrees. They would rather take a beating than be by themselves.

And lastly, these people are terrified of being criticized. They have very little ability to ask themselves whether or not the accusations which are made of them are in fact true. As I have written in my book *Overcoming Frustration and Anger* (published in the UK by Sheldon as *Calm Down*), accusations are really quite easy to manage if we simply ask ourselves if the accusations are true or false. If they are true, we agree with them and thank our accuser for pointing out our faults. But if the accusations are false, we simply ignore them.

Dependent people are sad and pathetic figures. Although they can be intelligent, attractive and skilled, it is still amazing to see how much they distrust their own abilities and lean upon others who are often no better at those skills than they are. That is a serious error, and they make it frequently.

Avoidant personality disorder

Avoidant personalities are very sensitive to rejection and criticism. They have very few friends, and generally stay away from people rather than get involved with them. This is reflected not only in their social activities, of course, but also in the way they try to avoid occupational activities that would bring them into greater contact with others. Even if they are quite good at their work, they tend to refuse advantageous promotions if these will get them more involved with others.

This social fear can get so bad that the subject simply feels unable to carry on a normal conversation for fear of asking dumb questions or being laughed at. I have known such individuals who were quite bright, highly educated, and yet who kept insisting that they didn't like talking to people because they 'wouldn't know what to talk about'. They rate themselves constantly by every little action they perform and, when they are not almost perfect, they feel humiliated, degraded and embarrassed. Then, when they know that they are showing their inferiority through signs of anxiety or blushing, they're even more uncomfortable.

As a result of these fears they rationalize wildly about why they can't go to a dance, why they can't start a business, why they can't ask for a raise, and why they can't call up someone for a social engagement. Life is simply too risky for them and they become certain that the best way to handle these frightening experiences is to avoid them.

When avoidant personalities follow their inclinations and avoid engaging with others they develop secondary problems on top of the fears they already had. For example, many become depressed, feel sorry for themselves over the empty lives they live, and become anxious, not only over social contacts but also over fear of failure, humiliation, injury and so on. And lastly, they become angry at themselves for failing to accomplish their goals. While their friends are enjoying life, they are looking on from the outside, all the while knowing deep in their hearts that they are largely responsible for their suffering and lack of companionship.

Only with a change in their self-ratings are they likely to alter their sad destinies. It is only natural that depression, anxiety and anger accompany the development of the avoidant personality. These people are very sensitive, enough surely to know how they are letting themselves down and generally making their lives miserable. As though this weren't enough, the avoidant personality can also develop full-blown phobias.

• Isn't that sad? Here we have people who don't like themselves. They expect rejection at every turn. They habitually avoid people. Then they easily add other painful emotions to their suffering – dependency disorders, paranoid disorders, schizoid personality disorders, and schizotypal personality disorders – and all for nothing.

To bring help to these suffering people often requires medication, but always requires counselling to reduce their inferiority feelings.

Paranoid personality disorder

The paranoid personality is the person who constantly expects to be exploited by others, has great distrust of his 'friends' or the loyalty of those close to him, and who constantly reads hidden messages in the most innocent remarks.

As if that weren't enough, the paranoid personality holds grudges for months or years, is unforgiving over slight insults and will not confide in people. This obviously cuts him off from those friendships and acquaintances which make life so beautiful.

The paranoid is also so sensitive that he or she is easily offended, makes insults out of the slightest innocent remark and tries to cure the situation by responding with anger, insults or sarcasm.

The last, but not least, consequence of negative self-ratings has to do with the usual tendency of paranoid people to become jealous and to constantly suspect their partners of being unfaithful. This is where loving relationships are almost always weakened or completely demolished.

Paranoid personalities need to understand that their problems are not caused by other people but by their own deep sense of inferiority and unworthiness. The cure for this problem is for them to stop being neurotically perfectionist, to develop their own skills, and to earn the respect of other people. But by being hostile, suspicious, super-sensitive, and secretive, it is practically impossible for them to develop that healthy sense of self-acceptance which makes all the difference in the world.

Negative self-rating is equivalent to a silent attack against yourself. When you do this to yourself for years you must of necessity have such a strong conviction of being undesirable that you perceive rejection in the actions of practically everyone you encounter. Since you reject yourself you cannot quite believe others will not reject you. This is internally consistent logic even though it is regrettably erroneous.

Once this massive negative self-rating is well established it sadly follows that you cannot believe that others find you desirable, that you are loved, and that people may still care for you even though you do not care for yourself. For this reason your insecurity breaks out in jealous rages and fear of losing your loved ones because you always feel inferior to all others.

And why shouldn't you believe this? You've worked overtime putting yourself down.

Schizoid personality disorder

When inferiority feelings do not lead to a paranoid personality disorder, they can easily lead to a schizoid personality disorder.

Schizoid personalities have a tendency to be indifferent to social relationships and are somehow not able to show their feelings in the normal way most people do. And because they are so unhappy in dealing with people they avoid intimacy, not just with their friends but also with their own family members. It follows, therefore, that they tend to be solitary and introvertive figures. We call them loners.

When they cut themselves off from social contacts they also cut themselves off from their feelings. It is therefore very difficult for them to show strong emotions. They have a neutral quality in their feelings, as though nothing ever means much. They do not feel great despair and they do not feel great joy. In their emotional life they are like robots.

Their sex lives are as poorly motivated as are their emotional lives. Since they are not eager for emotional intimacy, they are not eager for physical intimacy either. Can you begin to see the degree of dislike and distrust they have, not only for others, but for themselves? Much of this rejection of intimacy arises because of their deep conviction that they are simply undesirable. It follows therefore that, because they have shielded themselves so much against hurt, they are not accessible to normal criticism or to praise. By living behind a wall they avoid all manner of possible hurts. They have no close friends, no one to tell their deepest secrets to, and on those rare occasions when they do have someone to talk to it is generally only one person. The general feeling one has, then, for schizoid personalities is that they are very cold people, they live in a lonely world of their own, cut off from normal human contact. Within their invisible walls they simply don't feel the need to respond.

Since these people are so withdrawn they perhaps do not get into social conflict, even to the point that they no longer express aggression. But more than that, they appear absent-minded, they daydream, they have no clear-cut goals and they have difficulties dating. Thus, few of the males ever marry. Schizoid women, on the other hand, can be approached, and will accept dating passively, and then will marry.

Schizoid personalities work in jobs that do not require frequent contacts with others. If unemployed, they tend to move into the skid-row sections of cities where they live quiet and empty lives.

As chief psychologist at a mental hospital for five years, I had a number of schizoid clients. All of them, without exception, found it impossible to accept themselves, sometimes appallingly so. I'm certain many of them became isolated because of their severe self-ratings. The reverse, however, is equally plausible. If schizoid persons have a physical or genetic reason for this condition, then their sad lifestyles and their inability to achieve success and pleasure must surely also lead to low self-worth. Either way, they miss out on all that makes life a pleasure.

Schizotypal personality disorder

This condition is even more serious than the schizoid personality disorder. The symptoms are not those of a true schizophrenic but they are definitely headed in that direction. Schizotypal personalities appear odd in several ways, including speech, thought and behaviour. They explain events in terms of magic: 'Don't bother looking for the house keys, the door will be open when we arrive.' Or they have ideas of reference: 'Why are those people over there calling me a thief?' Or they have paranoid delusions: 'Everyone hates me and wants to poison my food.' They suffer from frequent illusions, which are errors they make when they explain what they perceive. For example, if a friend approached such an individual and greeted him with, 'Hi, Kirk,' the schizotypal personality might hear the words, 'Hi, jerk.'

A frequent sign, even more serious, is depersonalization, which means that the subject questions whether he or she has not changed into another person. Emotions which were formerly experienced now seem strange and unreal. Some feel they are living in a dream or a trance.

Their speech can become peculiar, ideas will be expressed in a confused manner, and the words they use will seem clearly out of place.

• Such people are often eccentric. Many of them bigots who are drawn to fringe religious cults. When under greater than usual stress they may function briefly at the psychotic level and show clear schizophrenic symptoms. Some evidence exists that more people become schizophrenics out of the schizotypal personality disorders than among the general population.

If you are wondering whether this condition applies to you, study the following list of symptoms. If you have any four you could be so diagnosed:

1. Magical thinking: this includes superstitions, clair-voyance, telepathy or a 'sixth sense'. In children, weird fantasies are common in this disorder.

2. Ideas of reference: schizotypal personalities believe that others talk negatively of them. This should come as no surprise since it clearly arises from inferiority feelings, a condition most disturbed people have.

3. Social isolation: a lack of close friends or people to confide in. Social contacts are confined to those needed for everyday demands for living.

4. Recurrent illusions: feeling the presence of someone who is not or cannot be present. Depersonalization (already described) and derealization, the feeling that the world is not real, are serious forms of these illusions.

5. Odd speech: characterized by an inability to organize thoughts or speak in a logical, sequential manner. Vagueness, overelaboration of speech fall under this heading as well.

6. Aloof and cold emotional style: avoidance of closeness and general inadequate social interaction.

7. Suspiciousness, jealousy, or paranoid ideas.

8. Unjustified anxiety in social conditions: hypersensitivity to rejection or criticism.

Please take note that there is a progression of severity of symptoms starting with the dependent personality, followed by the avoidant personality, then the paranoid personality, the schizoid personality and, finally, the most serious, the schizotypal personality disorder. I believe this progression depends largely, but not entirely, on the degree to which a person does not accept himself or herself. It is difficult to imagine some of these symptoms existing in people who do not put themselves down.

That's the difference self-acceptance makes.

3

The First Step:
Never Rate Yourself or Others

One of the saddest letters I have ever received from the readers of my books was from a young man in India. With shocking frankness he described himself as being a completely inferior person. There was nothing about himself which he admired. Everyone he compared himself to was superior. He was desperate to know what to do about this sad state of affairs.

I had the distinct feeling that nothing but the most massive change in attitude could ever bring him relief. My letter could only touch upon the strategies he would need to follow if he were ever to have peace of mind. The subject is simply too complex to explain in a letter and the strategies are much too difficult to follow from the brief explanation I could offer.

That event, however, is what set me to thinking of writing this book. Not enough has been written on this subject which addresses in a clear and concise manner how we can overcome inferiority feelings. I am convinced it is possible to do this once you learn what causes you to reject yourself and how you can avoid that no matter how you behave for the rest of your life. That's a tall order, I agree. However, if you accept the fact, as I do, that we are taught to feel inferior, then it is possible to teach people *not* to feel inferior. In other words, anything we can learn, we can unlearn.

There is only one technique you need to follow if you wish to avoid feelings of inferiority, low self-respect, low self-esteem, and low self-worth. To cure yourself of these conditions, do one thing: *never rate yourself or others*. Nothing else is needed. I will explain this technique in some detail in this chapter. However, I strongly suspect that you, the reader, will not be content with this method alone. You will wonder why I have ignored such techniques as confidence-building or assertiveness strategies. And, to a degree, you have a good point. All three methods will surely help. However, while teaching you to be a confident or assertive person will surely help you overcome inferiority feelings, neither is as good and as certain to work as avoiding all self-ratings. When you refuse to rate yourself over anything at anytime, you cannot feel inferior or lose self-respect no matter how you behave. That's something the other two methods cannot boast of. Peace of mind through never rating yourself depends on nothing but never rating yourself.

What is the self?

It is crucial that you fully understand this section. Until you do, all I have to say that follows will be confusing. Therefore, commit the definition of the self to memory. The self is *every conceivable thing about you that can be rated.*

There are clearly tens of thousands of ways your qualities can be rated. For example, I could rate your intelligence, strength or appearance as good or bad. But the same can be said for any qualities you have, such as honesty or generosity. That much is obvious. However, there are still thousands of other qualities which you or anyone could rate as being good or bad. The shape of your nose, the way your hair stands up, the fact that you have a squint or the fact that your hair is greying. Every thought you've ever had can be judged good or bad. Every deed you've ever done can be judged acceptable or unacceptable. In short, every conceivable good or bad thing that can be said about you, all added together, is the self. The self is never one or two or even a dozen properties, but many thousands. It just depends on how detailed you want to get.

Once you realize this fact, you will see much more easily why you can never rate the self. To make this point clearer, let me explain it in more detail.

Why you cannot logically rate yourself

Ratings are usually based on prejudice
A judge, sentencing a thief to jail, describes him as a danger to

the community. And yet the young man's parents hire a lawyer to get him leniency, while the mother tearfully proclaims her son is really a 'good boy'? Would she have said that about another mother's son if he had robbed her home? Hardly. This being the case, if we want to be rational people, we must admit that what or who we think is good or bad depends on what our relationship is to that thing or person. We overlook faults in our families, friends and countrymen but damn them if they are outside our families, or are strangers or foreigners. How much sense does that make?

We cannot logically judge people by a single trait

No one in his right mind would conclude that a whole barrel of apples is rotten because of one bad apple. And to say a mother is inferior or worthless because she screams at her child is to totally overlook the hundreds of kindnesses she also shows the child.

People cannot be judged by many traits

You will surely argue that if a mother beats her child, drinks heavily, and brings strange men home, she can certainly be rated as a bad person. The same objection again applies, even if we take a dozen more faults into consideration. We still cannot logically conclude she is bad. What are these serious complaints when compared to thousands of other traits we could praise?

Human traits are almost without number

When you come right down to it, to rate a person accurately, we would have to know him in great detail. First, we would need to know *all* of his good and bad qualities. However, to be sure we had got that right we would have to know how many qualities a person had to begin with. Then, if we knew the total number of good and bad traits there are, and the number of good and bad he had, then and only then could we decide that a certain person was good or bad. For then, don't you see, we could say he had 73.5% bad traits and 26.5% good traits. But as you shall see in a moment, not even that figure would tell us anything very accurate about a person.

Who could determine if a trait is good or bad?

Let's suppose we could list all the traits people have. We might then decide to set up a committee to determine what is a good trait and what is a bad trait. And where shall we find such a committee that would satisfy everyone's values?

Well, suppose we chose teachers. Or lawyers? How about ministers, or psychologists? Maybe we should have twenty people on such an important committee. Or would you want thirty, fifty, or a thousand? After all, if you're going to judge me as a good or bad writer, I want to make sure that I get an absolutely fair and correct judgment. But wait a moment. Even if we could agree that seven teachers, fifteen lawyers, eight ministers, six psychologists and five housewives should form this group, how would they be selected? If we choose these people from one area of the country we are obviously going to get a lopsided view of which traits are good or bad. To carry this point further, unless you used people from outside your own country you would only be getting a rating with a local or national flavour. Just think how you'd make out if you had committee members from Paris, Moscow, Tehran, South Africa and the United States. Would they rate you differently than a committee from rural Spain. You bet they would. Again, can you see how futile it is to attempt to rate people by their characteristics?

Traits change constantly

When you say you are 5 feet 8 inches high and you're 21 years old you are making an observation that has a fair amount of reliability to it. However, if you label your self as a hard worker, we can have less faith in that statement because we may judge that trait differently from you. Maybe you work hard during the week but sleep all weekend. Maybe you work hard only when the boss is watching or if you're being paid extra.

Honesty, kindness, humour, meanness, and many other character traits are of a situational nature. That means they change depending upon the circumstances of the moment. Your height doesn't change, and your weight doesn't change much, but your trait of friendliness, for example, could change from one hour to the next – you might be very chummy Saturday morning while playing golf with your friends, but turn hostile that afternoon as you sit trying to read the paper in your backyard while the neighbours' kids are screaming and shouting in theirs.

I'm afraid it makes no sense to judge anyone by traits that change from hour to hour or day to day. I vaguely recall reading about a man who worked in a concentration camp as a warden and was so cruel he was referred to as 'The Beast'. After the war he fled to another country and worked in a hospital. He changed so much as a hospital orderly he was referred to as 'The Saint'.

Traits cannot be weighed consistently

If all of the previous objections could be overcome, there would remain one final one which is never likely to be corrected. I'm referring to our need to recognize that some personality traits are better than others, but we never know by how much.

For example if I compare your trait of honesty to your friend's trait of bravery, who is the better person? If we could agree to make the judgment only on one trait we would now have to decide which trait was the more important.

Is honesty more important than bravery? If so, is it 1.75 times better, or 17.4 times, or only 0.005 times better? We don't have the foggiest idea.

If you are in the habit of saving money, phoning your mother once a week or adopting stray cats, and I compare these habits to your friend's habits of keeping physically fit, mowing his lawn once a week, and attending church faithfully, unless we can determine *how* good it is to do any of these things, we can't arrive at a meaningful comparison.

The upshot of this analysis is: you cannot logically rate yourself or others by traits, behaviours, possessions or talents. As these several observations clearly show, you have no business ever judging people or yourself by a few or even many traits. You can never rationally say: 'Roger is a good man.' That's too vague. You have to be *specific* when you make such judgments, for only then are they helpful in understanding what we want to express. Roger may be good all right, but at *what*? Is he a good golfer? When? He was a good golfer last week when he played on Saturday between 9 and 11.30 a.m. He was a poor golfer when he played again a week later.

All people with inferiority feelings use labels to explain behaviour. The worst labels are probably these: good, bad, superior, inferior. Avoid them always when you use them as ratings of persons, as in: 'He's a better person than you are', 'You're inferior', 'I'm no good.' Don't make such sweeping statements. Be specific. How are you inferior? You're superior in which particular way? Be precise. You're better than Betty, not totally and forever, but only when it comes to playing bridge. Six months from now Freddie may be a superior bridge player (not a superior person) to Betty.

There you have the mechanics of self-rating and other-rating. This is how we develop inferiority and superiority feelings, not just of specific qualities we possess, but of the whole person. It is one of the most unhealthy acts you can commit against yourself or others. Painful emotional disturbances result from rating persons rather than behaviour.

Terry London, in his new book *A Challenge to Change* (1988) said it best: 'rating or measuring your self or your ego will tend to make you anxious, miserable and ineffective. By all means, rate your acts and try (undesperately) to do well. For you may be happier, healthier, richer or more achievement-confident (confident that you can achieve) if you perform adequately. But you will not be, nor had you better define yourself as, a better person.'

Emotional disturbances created by self-rating

If you have ever rated people instead of things *about* people, and you have done the same for yourself, I can guarantee that you have suffered from some or all of the following disturbances: anger, jealousy, conceit, fear, shame, guilt, embarrassment, humiliation and insult.

Depression

As I previously explained in an earlier book, *Depression*, this emotion is caused by self-blame, self-pity and other-pity. Only the first method (self-blame) is caused by self-rating.

To feel guilty, you must believe two conditions are true:

1. That you did something bad, sinful or disgusting.
2. That you are bad, evil and undesirable because you behaved badly.

The first condition is, of course, often true. After all, who's perfect? We all behave unacceptably at times, quite often as a matter of fact. However, if you will not label yourself as *being* bad for doing wrong, you will never *feel* guilty or inferior, you will only be admitting that you did wrong. Then you can change your behaviour more easily because you won't be distracted by painful guilt feelings. Try always to distinguish *feeling* guilty from *being* guilty. If you back your car into your neighbour's hedge you're correct to say you *are* guilty of destroying property. But you have no business *feeling* guilty, that is, rating yourself as a good-for-nothing human being because you were momentarily a poor driver.

Am I suggesting that we never blame ourselves for anything (that is *feel* guilty)? Absolutely. You have a moral obligation to forgive yourself for every error or unkind thing you have ever done or will ever do.

'But,' you ask, 'how can I convince myself of that?'

There are three reasons why we have the right always to accept ourselves as imperfect human beings who *will* make small or large mistakes.

Deficiency

We are fragile people and simply cannot do everything we would like. Some of us are strong, some can compose music, others can cook. However, most cannot be outstanding in more than one or a few activities.

If you lose your job because you cannot type fast enough, it may be that you don't have the fine coordination of eye and hand which such work requires. To label yourself as a dunce or a failure as a result is unfair and leaves you without respect.

Actually, all you've proved is that you are an unsatisfactory typist on a *particular* job, for *that* particular boss, on *that* particular day. You are not a bad person. You are a slow typist because you don't have the talent.

Ignorance

But suppose you do have the coordination needed for typing but never learned to type correctly? Perhaps you type with two fingers instead of ten. Does that mean you're bad because you're obviously an inferior employee? How much sense does it make to hate yourself just because you have never learned to do the job right? Ignorance is a perfectly valid reason to forgive yourself for your errors. Blaming yourself, however, is perfectly ridiculous. Can you fly a plane, play an oboe or speak Icelandic? No? Oh, I see, you must be evil. Right? Rubbish. Think that way if you like, my friend. As for me, I will never put myself down for doing badly at anything if I was never taught to do better.

Disturbance

Let's get back to our secretary. Only this time she comes to the office with plenty of talent for typing, she's learned to type 100 words a minute, but her baby is sick, her husband is drunk, and the landlord wants his back rent. She's stressed and makes more mistakes in one day than she normally makes in a month.

Is she bad? If so, every unhappy and stressed person who ever got a parking ticket, yelled at the kids, or forgot to make an important phone call is also bad. Again, rubbish. Disturbance is a perfectly sane reason for forgiving ourselves for our faulty behaviour. We simply can't be very efficient if we are angry, depressed, afraid or jealous.

Many of you will protest that people will feel free to commit endless sins since they won't have to feel guilty if they follow this advice. Not so. People commit *more* errors when they hate themselves. The fact that they are already feeling badly about themselves means they will want to punish themselves even more. One of the best ways to do that is to behave badly again. What a solution!

Anger

To get angry you have to believe that you're right, that the other person is wrong, and that he or she must agree with you and do as you demand. In short, you are acting like a hysterical child when you get angry since you think the world and everyone in it must do as you say whether they like it or not. If you didn't have that sense of superiority, that feeling that only what you think or want counts, you couldn't get angry at all.

People with so-called high self-esteem can justify anger easily. All those people beneath them in intelligence, education, wealth, or talent are merely peasants and don't deserve respect.

Therefore, let us be good models for others and not act like stuck-up, conceited and grandiose people by not allowing them to be human beings while we act as though we are above fault.

In Chapter 5, on assertiveness, I will go into the dynamics of anger more deeply.

Fear

Those of you who are forever putting yourselves down almost always develop a host of fears. How could it be otherwise? When you have convinced yourself you're the scum of the earth, how can you be expected to lead a revolution? For that matter, how could you finish your education, get married, run for office, or be invited to the neighbourhood picnic?

When you say you are afraid of people, or afraid of accidents, you are really saying that you are weak and powerless and are not brave enough or strong enough to face any danger. You are like a cork on the ocean, bobbing up and down and blown in any direction the wind takes it. That is the fate of the person who fears life.

How much better it is to face our fear so that we can remove it. Even the worst cowards among us have shown many moments of courage in the course of their lives. We crossed the street on our way to school. We drove the car in heavy traffic. We married and took on the responsibility of raising a family. And still we treat ourselves like frightened children. It doesn't make sense, does it?

If someone threatened your family, you otherwise fearful people would fight wildcats to protect them, wouldn't you? But you're supposed to be timid, remember? How do we account for such courage? Obviously, if you think an issue is important enough, you will overcome your fear. Isn't that interesting? Here you are, feeling like an unworthy person, afraid to enter a room full of strangers, labouring under the weight of massive inferiority feelings and low self-esteem, but you still manage to rise above this fault if the issue is important enough, and you suddenly don't care what others think of you. Nice going.

Jealousy

The jealous person makes three incorrect judgments when his lover enjoys the company of others. First, he concludes he is justified in feeling threatened. His sense of being unworthy or desirable is so strong that he concludes he will practically always be inferior to the people whom his loved one likes to seek out. If those people are very young or very old they present no threat to the jealous person. But if they are attractive, humorous, bright or talented, watch out. The jealous person senses he is in a dangerous situation. Why? Because he has *no trust in himself* and in his ability to compete successfully against these intruders.

What makes him panic so easily at the approach of any capable person? It is his deep sense of insignificance. How else can we explain his reactions to wanting his partner never to talk to anyone? If he had a healthy view of himself it would not occur to him to get so upset.

The second error the jealous person makes is that if his partner found someone superior to him, this new person would tempt his partner to leave him. How ridiculous! None of us is the best at everything. We all know people who are more attractive, more fun, more talented or more wealthy than our partners, but how often do we adults desert each other? Certainly it happens, but hardly as often as the jealous person fears. If he would just reflect a few moments, he could easily see how unrealistic these concerns are when he realizes he, too, has met interesting people but not left his partners on that account.

The jealous person's third error of judgment and quite a serious one too, is to conclude that he cannot stand rejection, that rejection hurts, and that he cannot live without his lover. No wonder he wants to control every moment of her life.

If these views were truly sensible, I could well understand his fright and his need to monitor every phone call, every glance and every evening out. But they are not. If you are like this jealous person, you need to change your ideas drastically so that you can relax. Remember that rejection *can* be tolerated. No one upsets you unless you choose to be upset. Granted, it is no fun to lose your partner, but it's not the end of the world either. You're not a child. You're a mature adult and don't *need* to be loved. You *want* love, of course, but you don't have to have it, not anymore.

The lesser symptoms of inferiority

I want it clearly understood that I am using the term 'inferiority complex' to mean the same as 'low self-esteem'. Don't protest that they are not the same. They are. Sometimes my client will admit to having low self-esteem and still deny he has any feelings of inferiority. One is not possible without the other. Both terms mean that you have rejected yourself, that you have compared yourself negatively with others, and that you are therefore simply an undesirable and unworthy as a person.

The less serious symptoms of negative self-rating which practically everyone experiences from time to time are shame, embarrassment, humiliation, shyness and feeling insulted. These emotions are obviously fairly similar. However, if we choose, we can define them in slightly different ways, depending on the intensity of discomfort we experience over our behaviours or those of other people.

Suppose you went to a party with your friend. He or she drank too much and behaved badly. If that behaviour involved your friend being merely loud and somewhat unruly, it would certainly be appropriate for you and your hostess to feel annoyance and disapproval. However, most people, being overly sensitive, and all of them struggling with self-rating, would also feel embarrassment.

If the friend was more than merely annoying, and the hostess was angry over the advances your friend made toward other guests, you might also feel anger yourself, perhaps even humiliation.

However, if your friend actually damaged a piece of furniture and threw up on the hostess's rug, you might now feel shame.

The hostess, meanwhile, in addition to feeling these degrees of discomfort, would surely insist she was insulted that your friend had behaved so badly in her home. You might perhaps also feel insulted by your friend's behaviour.

If your friend has normal sensitivities, he or she is also likely to feel (after sobering up) the same feelings of embarrassment, humiliation and shame.

I have described normal behaviour for all three persons. But what about healthy behaviour? Healthy behaviour requires very different responses from each person. The hostess has no business whatever feeling anything more than annoyance and irritation. Why should she (or you, for that matter) feel embarrassment, humiliation or shame when neither she nor you did anything wrong? Your friend drank too much. Not the hostess, not you. Just because you went to the party with your friend doesn't mean you behaved badly too. And just because your friend disrupted the hostess's party there is no justification for the hostess to take the incident personally. She had nothing to do with it. We are not responsible for the behaviours of others, even when they are close to us.

Now, what about your friend? Will he or she feel guilt and shame? Probably. This is a mistake. Your friend need not lose any self-respect, or feel the slightest bit inferior. He or she is imperfect. Getting drunk at a party is clearly imperfect behaviour. Your friend must not judge himself or herself as inferior on the basis of one thoughtless act. He or she is still a decent person, usually courteous, hard-working, loving, civil, humorous, and so on. We cannot rate people, only things about people.

Does that mean the hostess should totally ignore this rude behaviour? Of course not. The hostess would help your friend if she wrote or spoke to him or her, expressing concern over his or her recovery, and then did not invite that person to another party for a long time or ever again. That, ladies and gentlemen, is the best response. It is firm *and* kind.

A word about shyness. Current research suggests shyness may be genetic to some degree. If so, there is little you can do about it except to push yourself into social situations when it is expected of you and then give yourself some time to be alone so you can recover. Since this is a condition you inherited, you will not be likely to control it to a normal degree unless you work at it vigorously. Even then, many shy people will hardly ever be as comfortable in a large group as they are in a small group.

The trouble with self-love

We are repeatedly told that loving ourselves is the best cure for low self-esteem. Sounds reasonable, doesn't it? But wait. To love yourself when you act morally, for example, means you will hate yourself if you behave immorally. Do you now see why all self-ratings are wrong? You simply can't lead a stable life if you hate yourself one minute and love yourself the next. It is much better to avoid all self-ratings and accept yourself unconditionally. If we are not bad people because we behave badly, then we are not good people because we behave nobly.

Self-acceptance – the best solution

We come now to the heart of this chapter. When all is said and done, the very best thing you can do about your good and bad points is to change them if you can, or accept them as they are for the present or for ever. When you accept yourself you do precisely the opposite of what most people do, which is to rate themselves.

Self-acceptance says you may not like your looks but you won't dislike yourself over them.

Self-acceptance says you may severely disapprove of the way you raised your children but you will not judge yourself as an evil or horrible person because you were an abusive parent. We cannot rate people by their actions, appearance, talents or possessions. Remember that always.

Self-acceptance says that you can never lose face, feel shame or be embarrassed if you refuse to rate yourself along with your qualities.

Asians, and to a lesser degree Europeans and Americans, truly believe that they lose respect for themselves if they are laughed at, if their names are printed in the newspaper over a family quarrel, or if they deserve criticism of any kind. But to believe in the whole idea of 'losing face' makes you an instant pawn of other people's opinions. You are their slave. Your value as a person is in their hands and whether you will feel like holding your head up high today or slink off into a corner depends on every Tom, Dick and Harry. That's no way to go through life.

Why should you accept the judgments of others? True, people are usually fairly accurate about judging our skills, looks, or possessions, but they are never right when they make that second judgment about us which says we are *good or bad people* because of our skills, looks or possessions. When you feel you have lost face, you have agreed with both of those decisions from others, that you cook badly, for instance, and that you, therefore, are an undesirable person.

You can accept their judgement if you choose to do so. However, if you do, then it is you who is making you lose face, not others. What others say about us is relatively harmless. What *we* say about ourselves can be uplifting or very painful.

To avoid all these ugly and confusing complications that go along with rating yourself, why not make up your mind to stop rating yourself and others and see what it's like to live with a truly sane philosophy for a change. From this day forward, never hate yourself, never love yourself, instead accept yourself. This also applies to others. Never hate others, and never love others. Accept others as they are, or try to change them if you can. Then, if they can still satisfy your deepest desires and needs, you will love all the wonderful things they do for you. You will not think they are better persons than others simply because they make you very happy.

In a nutshell

It is not easy to understand why self-rating is not in your best interest. After all, it goes totally against our usual ways of thinking about people and their behaviours. I hope the following summary of what I've said so far makes it all a little clearer:

1. Teach your children *not* to strive for high self-esteem. This is nothing less than teaching them arrogance, conceit and superiority feelings.

2. Teach your children never to rate themselves negatively. That leads to guilt, depression, feelings of inferiority and insecurity.

3. Instead, urge your children to seek *self-acceptance*. That avoids all self-rating and the wide sweep of emotions from conceit to self-hate.

4. All statements of self-esteem are statements of over-generalization since most of the qualities we possess are ignored in favour of the ones we happen to focus on for the moment.

5. The self refers to millions of characteristics. It cannot be measured by fewer than all the traits which go to make up the self.

6. When you refuse to rate your self you avoid all feelings of guilt and inferiority. Both lead to depression by self-blame.

7. When you refuse to rate others, you avoid all anger and its many forms: resentment, bitterness, hate, aggression and fury.

8. Self-rating is unhealthy, painful, grandiose and wrong. You cannot be a contented human being until you accept your strengths and weaknesses for the present, change what you can, and accept what you can't.

9. To love yourself is to rate yourself and will only give you trouble when what you want is security.

10. Psychological health is achieved most fully by

performing three operations: rating things *about* people, but never rating people themselves; developing your skills to the maximum (see Chapter 4); and making others respect you (see Chapter 5).

11. When you are told you are bad, your response had better be 'At what?' Always be specific, never general or global.

12. In short, leave your self alone. Then how do you rate yourself? You don't. *Accept yourself.*

13. Finally, try never to feel embarrassed, humiliated, insulted or ashamed. They are all varieties of self-rating and give you away instantly as an insecure person.

Recipe for self-acceptance

In an earlier book I wrote a short prescription for self-acceptance. I'd like to share it with you:

Hold your head up high and fill your heart with hope. Do not let the pessimism of the world drown you in messages of despair. You are a member of the human race, the most spectacular achievement in our world. Though you are imperfect, you are far more gifted than you are faulty.

Accept yourself with your shortcomings if you cannot alter them. With guidance and hard work, however, you can reduce your weaknesses and your flaws to a point where they do not interfere with your enjoyment of life.

Stop neglecting yourself. You are not much good to others if you are not good to yourself. Hold your head up high, for you are one of a kind. Be proud that even with your limitations you have enough talent, intelligence, and resources to fulfil your destiny to a reasonable degree.

Hold your head up high and face the world with curiosity and gentleness. More often than not others will respond in kind. But if they should not, then do not hesitate to become firm with them, knowing deep in your heart that these are not bad people, they are like you, merely imperfect. But because you value yourself, you will not allow them to abuse you.

However many years you have left on this earth, use them well. Satisfy your deepest desires and needs to a reasonable degree. And always give yourself the attention and the care you would give those you love the most. To show respect for others but not yourself makes a mockery of your best intentions. Teach others the morality of self-acceptance by setting an example of it in yourself.

4

The Second Step:
Develop Performance-Confidence

If you recall my comments about the self being *everything* about you, and that we can never rate the complete self by a few traits, then you will realize why we can't use the word 'self-confidence' and still make sense. To say you have *self*-confidence, would be to imply that you trust yourself to be able to do *everything* extremely well – in other words, that you are perfect.

It therefore makes much more sense to refer to your ability to handle yourself socially, for example, as having *social* confidence, not self-confidence. The former means only that you know how to make friends, not that you are better than others who can't make friends.

In this way we can refer to other areas of human activity and, in doing so, rate not the person, only the person's performances. Again, for this reason, it is more logical to avoid the term 'self-confidence' entirely since it makes no sense, and to use the term '*performance*-confidence' instead to refer to our actual behaviours in various activities. If we want to be more specific we can always use such terms as *love*-confidence, *work*-confidence, *academic*-confidence, and so on.

Unfortunately it will take people a long time to acquire this habit. Even though they will be wrong logically to conclude that they are better than others because they are better *at some tasks* compared to others, they will still do so. Their self-ratings will leap sky high and they will feel great – all for the wrong reasons.

I urge you not to rate your self by your performance and to use your performance-confidence to give you the courage to learn many things well, not to feel superior as a person over others.

Keeping this in mind, let me show you how to improve your

performance through making yourself achieve your goals rather than avoid them.

Too many people think they must be outstanding in at least one activity to feel proud of themselves. Only if they can achieve recognition of unusual magnitude do these people feel worthy. How sad. It is most regrettable that such rigid standards are held up as the measure of personal success. If this is accurate then most of us lesser mortals are unworthy. This is hardly a just view.

Those who are so demanding of themselves are often neurotically concerned about their performances. Perfectionists are often very unhappy and insecure people. Why? Because perfectionists are also imperfect. It is most ironic that those people who are seldom satisfied with anything short of near-perfection are often the sad victims of this dangerous philosophy. Why do I use such a strong term as 'dangerous'? Simply because so many demands are made of the human system (when perfectionism is sought) that it simply can't keep up.

Take the case of students who believe they must achieve top grades in every class every year. The only solutions to this dilemma are to work so hard that top grades are almost always achieved, or to decide that perfectionism is neither healthy nor necessary, or to risk an emotional breakdown.

The cardinal problem and weakness with perfectionism is that it does not lead to work-confidence and self-acceptance *unless* it is achieved. But then, who's perfect? Let confidence grow out of making the attempt, not out of the achievement. The climb up the mountain can bring as much pride and satisfaction as actually reaching the top.

I am repeatedly asked by my clients what they can do to develop a sense of confidence. My answer is always the same: 'Do what interests you. Work at it no matter how badly you do it. Learn by your mistakes and try again. That leads to improvement – not perfection. Practice does not make perfect, it makes the master.

The principles of performance-discipline

There are five principles of performance-discipline which, if you practise them diligently, will help you develop skills and talents you never believed you had.

Don't procrastinate

First, generally pay more attention to long-range consequences than to short-range benefits. If you always put immediate pleasures before delayed pleasures you will probably end up being a miserable person.

Among the unhappiest people I have ever encountered are those who would never deny themselves a good time and would repeatedly give in to their temptations, only to suffer serious frustrations and disappointments in the future.

Those students who would rather watch TV, play sports, or spend hours on the phone with friends pay dearly for avoiding their homework. Those who will not avoid high-calory foods and who won't exercise three to four times a week will surely enjoy their ice cream and cake but will feel self-conscious about the bulges in their figures which might keep them from socializing. One of my clients, an attractive young lady, could simply not be tempted by her pleading husband to attend parties or even go shopping because she had gained more weight than she wanted others to see.

All that I have thus far said seems obvious enough, or so it would seem. The problem with people who give into temptations without regard for the distant consequences is that they actually believe giving into temptation truly leads to greater happiness. It does not, at least not always.

'Surely', you might protest, 'there are times when not disciplining ourselves is a rational action?'

The answer is clearly: 'Yes, if you don't expect to live very long. If you're going to die in a few weeks why in heaven's name would you not want to play, drink, smoke, and eat everything you ever lusted for? But, if you're betting on the odds, you'll probably live until your seventies. That means you'll have years to live with the mistakes you make today.'

All of us need time to fool around and take breaks from our

strict schedules. 'All work and no play makes Johnny a dull boy', as the folk wisdom goes. That's why soldiers take ten-minute breaks every hour, and why we go home earlier on Friday, and why we enjoy holidays and vacations. Without these rests we could get too carried away with the notion of discipline and literally work ourselves to death. This condition, known in Japan as *karoshi*, describes what has been happening to the current generation of Japanese middle-management employees. Some have been working over 90 hours a week for months and years on end. The result: in 1988 about 400 Japanese males worked themselves to death.

Leaving such abuse aside, the principle – that facing problems is usually better for us than avoiding them – still holds. It is the most important of all the five principles of performance-discipline.

Settle for less than perfect

After you have mastered the tendency to procrastinate you are ready for the next step toward building performance-confidence; not quitting when you start out doing poorly. That state of affairs, doing badly for a long time as you work your way to mastery, is the second most important technique to success.

The root of this problem is impatience. Any skill of any complexity takes time to learn, lots of time. Someone I know gave up painting after doing two pictures. Did he actually expect to do well on his second attempt? Apparently he did because he gave up his goal in disgust and was completely convinced he'd never be able to paint well.

We have all been brainwashed into believing that 'if it's worth doing, it's worth doing well'. Another equally erroneous version is 'if you can't do it right, don't do it at all'. If we take these folk wisdoms literally we are left with nothing but blowing our noses or picking our teeth. How can this reflect reality? Did we not all fumble as we learned to walk, talk, or use a knife and fork? Did we not appear clumsy and self-conscious when first learning to dance?

These examples are surely so apparent that they are not very convincing. Yet, the same problem is present when parents discipline children. Until they have their second or third child they make a number of mistakes which can be corrected only by trial and error. Would we tell inexperienced parents to give their first child away because they were making mistakes in their parenting?

When we accept the philosophy that it is more important to do than to do well (as is repeatedly pointed out by Cognitive-Behavioural therapists) we will become fearless in our pursuit of our goals. What, then, can stop us as we learn to invest our finances, to change our self-defeating habits through psychotherapy, to persevere as we exercise to stay youthful, or to refuse to give up at improving our sports or artistic and musical skills which provide endless moments of satisfaction?

This may sound like a trivial issue. You may wonder what happens to people who give up if their high standards are not met. I can think of a number of serious examples, but let me mention only a few.

One gentleman came to me because he could not bring himself to finish his thesis for his PhD in biology. The research had already been done. The first two chapters were typed and pleased him reasonably well. It was while writing his third chapter that he ran into trouble. He was unhappy with it and didn't know how to correct the problem. Instead of finishing his chapter as best he could (so he could have a third chapter to polish up later, as I suggested), he made the mistake of repeatedly rewriting the chapter from the start, thus never finishing it. He, alas, stoutly believed he had to do it 'right' or reject it totally. I regret to report I was not able to convince him that to do something in an inferior manner is far better than not doing anything at all. I think of him from time to time and wonder if he ever achieved his degree.

In the final analysis he was a victim of the mentality so prevalent in many cultures that being first, being top gun, the best, the winner, is all that counts. Being second doesn't count. Doing well can't begin to bring the satisfaction that doing brilliantly can, or so it is believed. As a result, my client and all those talented and hard-working people all over the world who gave up because they were second best lose confidence in their skills and lost their sense of humour in the bargain. How very sad.

Finish what you start, no matter the level of success. You will learn by your mistakes. With enough feedback you will eventually discover the secrets of a fine performance and with it you will find your performance-confidence rising along with your self-acceptance.

Tiny steps

The size of a task has a great deal to do with the probability of its being completed. Small tasks are handled briefly, large tasks are left unfinished. Not always, of course. The youngster whose duty it is to take out the garbage, or feed the dog – neither requiring more than a few minutes – often requires repeated warnings from others. In the main, however, it is true that we tend to finish tasks that can be completed quickly but procrastinate shamefully if they require days or years. Women manage to prepare meals daily but struggle to start spring house cleaning because it calls for work which can last weeks.

That is no way to acquire performance-confidence. Work which is unfinished or skills which are only partly refined leave us unhappy. We are dissatisfied with our incompleteness. Our unfinished labours demonstrate nothing except our laziness.

One of the best ways to help you finish what you start is to break it down into jobs of whatever size is necessary to avoid giving up. Psychological research has for many years indicated that distributed practice is often superior to mass practice. This means, for example, that a long poem can more easily be memorized if learned a few stanzas at a time rather than all at once. Divide a 1000 page book into 10 pages a night and the book can be read leisurely and with pleasure in 100 days. With ease one can read three such books in a year and have time left over.

This book was written a page a day, as were the thirteen I wrote before it. If I care to write more at weekends, all the better. In any event, this practice has enabled me to write approximately a book a year for over a dozen years.

My clients have been able to repair their homes, install

bathroom fans, change the oil in their cars, and write Christmas cards, all with this technique. It is so easy, so simple, and so painless it surprises me that I have to teach it at all. But teach it I am compelled to do.

So you're not impressed with writing Christmas cards or changing the oil in a car? I agree, these are hardly earth-shattering achievements. However, suppose you use this technique to develop an exercise programme that keeps you aerobically fit. You develop it a bit at a time, working at it a few minutes during the beginning stage and expanding it by a few push-ups and a few extra deep knee bends as the weeks pass. You keep this up and, little by little, eventually you get to the point where you are fitter than you have ever been. That's not insignificant stuff, ladies and gentlemen, that could be life-saving.

In addition, as you gradually progress toward your goal, never forget the other reward from your performance-discipline. That reward is a gradual reduction of anxiety in just plain living. As you master life's challenges little step by little step; as you persevere and refuse to give up merely because you have not reached perfection, you become more comfortable with life itself.

That is why there is such a thing as the Olympics for the disabled. Participants race in wheelchairs, run marathons on crutches, not because this is fun but because life is less frightening to people who master these obstacles. They develop sports-confidence along with callouses. And their proudest moments come from their victories.

Study the feedback

The fourth crucial technique which is needed if you are going to develop a high level of confidence is to be able to learn from experience. In the final analysis it is practically the only way some people ever learn anything. It is very rare that we can observe a certain behaviour and repeat it without a mistake unless it is terribly simple in nature. An exception is the case of a young blind man who simply sat down at the piano once as a child and began to play without ever having had any instruction. Not only that, he also had the ability to hear a musical composition and then play it note for note correctly the first time. This is, of course, a degree of genius which we simply do not understand. Most behaviours, to be performed in an acceptable manner, must be demonstrated and repeated at least a few times and often thousands of times.

But this statement is not entirely correct either. Repetition is not the ingredient which makes for improvement. It is perfectly possible to do a task over and over and still keep repeating the same mistake until you die. Practice does not make you perfect, it makes you the master, but only if you *learn* by the practice. To learn by practice means to study your performance very carefully, to analyse it for its strong and weak points, and to decide how to change the performance on the next occasion. That's why the old saying, 'Practice makes perfect', should be amended to say, 'The analysis of errors, and the practice of new behaviour, make for mastery'. Unfortunately that's not a catchy phrase and it will probably never catch on. But therein, nevertheless, lies the essence of the way people improve. Again, this surely sounds like a self-evident statement to you, and you may possibly object to the obviousness of this material. Let me assure you, it is not obvious. Practically every one of you who is reading this book right now has recently made an error and you made very little note of what you did wrong and what you would have to do the following time. It is my observation that people do not change because of their negative experiences nearly as much as they could *if they analysed these experiences.*

I have counselled men and women who have remarried, often more than once, essentially the same kinds of people they married the first time. How many of you have lost friends because you did not change your negative behaviour? How many of you have had difficulty in your jobs because you did not change your habit of being tardy, or gossiping, or giving the boss a bad time? How many of you have an addiction to alcohol or narcotics or to shopping or sex and know that you are injuring yourself every time you perform those compulsive behaviours but still you don't stop? How many of you have locked yourselves out of your car and never come up with a fool-proof method by which you could avoid that embarrassment in the future? How many of you are very poor at remembering names and have never asked yourself what you could do the next time to improve your memory? And there are dozens and dozens of other examples which prove that we simply don't learn just by our experience.

If we don't learn by experience (by asking ourselves what we did right and what we did wrong) then how can we improve our experience the next time? How can we get better at something if we simply have an experience, take the consequences for our errors, do not change our behaviours and then make the same mistakes? Smart people don't do that. The intelligent thing, of course, is to calmly think over our problem behaviour, analyse it very carefully, find out that we did wrong and then try not to repeat those same errors. But this takes considerable effort.

Normally we notice instead what we do wrong, we think we'll make the necessary changes the next time, but we haven't gone through a careful study as to exactly what the problem was and what we intend to do the following time. Let me show you what needs to be done if you really want to learn by your experience.

First, when you see what your error is, stop what you are doing and express it in plain language. One of my clients unfortunately and frequently had bad breath and, since he was a salesman, it was important that he have his breath fresheners with him whenever he made a call. On one occasion when he was to talk to an important client, he searched his car glove compartment for the freshener but realized that he had put it in his jacket pocket the last time he used it, and that it was probably in the suit hung in his closet at home.

So far so good. He at least knows what the problem is. Now he must figure out how he intends to solve this problem so it won't happen again. My client then bought two rolls of mouth fresheners and placed one in his brief case and the other in his glove compartment.

He then realized that that was not good enough because he could have avoided the whole problem had he checked his pockets before hanging up his suit. He decided then and there he would always pat all his pockets, not only in his trousers but also in his jacket, before hanging them up. In this way he would probably not have this difficulty again. In fact, it worked exactly that way.

This is a minor example of how one corrects annoying slips in behaviour that create frustrations.

Another one of my clients tried to rely heavily upon his memory. Being a busy man, and therefore being easily distracted with any number of issues that came up any day of the week, he often lost his train of thought and would totally forget what he had to do.

I suggested to him that he think of a solution which was foolproof and which he could employ instantly. In less than a few minutes he had the thought that if he did not have pencil and paper handy but could get to a telephone, he'd simply phone in the item that he wanted to remember to his answering machine at his office and leave it up to his secretary to pass the note on to him and place it on his desk. That cured the problem completely.

The same applies to your general growth and emotional control. Every time you get depressed, feel inferior, feel guilty, angry, jealous, or what have you, the same principle applies. Ask yourself what you did to get into that situation and what you have to do the following time to avoid it. In this way we mature, we change our personalities for the better because we simply aren't saying to ourselves 'I got angry and I wish I hadn't. I better not do that again or my boss will fire me.'

That's not good enough. You also want to say, 'I got angry and I don't want that to happen again. But what made me get angry in the first place? I must have changed one of my desires and made a demand out of it. Which desire was it? It was that the boss would give me Saturday off. He didn't do that. Then I changed the wish into a demand and insisted that he had to do what I wanted him to do. That's the problem. I have to remind myself that I don't have to have everything I want, that the world doesn't belong to me, that not everybody can treat me fairly, and that if I want something, I don't have to have it. I am not a child and other people, because they are imperfect, have a right to make mistakes and be unfair whether I like it or not.'

Do you see the difference between that final solution and the previous one? The first states the problem. But the second states the problem *and* comes up with a plausible solution. And if a plausible solution does not work, then get back to the drawing board and rework the whole issue until you find a solution that works for you.

All of this is done for the explicit purpose of building up your performance-confidence, reducing the mistakes you make throughout any one day, and making life more enjoyable for yourself and for others. And as you do so it is easy to see that your sense of life-confidence will improve and with that your inferiority feelings will lessen.

Therefore, start taking note of your mistakes but also start deciding what you want to do about them. Come up with a plan and then implement that plan. If you did that with most of your irritating behaviours you would be surprised at how efficient a person you would soon become.

Reward yourself, penalize yourself

Be sure that you do not give up because of boredom, that ever-present killer of motivation. Be prepared to get bored. It's practically unavoidable if you have to stay at a learning task for a matter of months or years.

To avoid boredom, understand first what boredom is. Boredom arises when behaviour is not rewarded. But, if any activity is made to seem pleasant, fun, or gratifying every so often, it squeezes out boredom every time.

Therefore, when you feel like quitting, reward yourself for what you have already accomplished. Do this in any way that works for you. For example, if your task is to paint all the rooms of your home, then, when the job gets too dull to continue, stop for a short while. But then take pride in what you have accomplished thus far. Even if you only did one wall of one room, that's at least done and you're that much closer to completion. Taking a break is the reward to give yourself for working just to the point of boredom.

It is not wise to work straight on and disregard your boredom too often because you will turn a pleasant or neutral task into a negative one. If you do that too often you simply won't finish the job.

You can reward yourself with a special pleasure or a bonus whenever you finish a room. In this way you can propel yourself into higher motivation, which may be all it takes to finish your job. Take a night off whenever you finish a room. Treat yourself to a fine meal, or an evening out, or something else you'd enjoy. The best rewards, however, are often not material ones but kind words of praise. That's right, you can reward yourself endlessly and efficiently, without spending a penny, if you will only talk approvingly to yourself.

When you begin to feel bored, tell yourself you are doing fine, the boredom won't last forever, every effort brings you closer to the end, and even though you've wanted to throw in the towel a number of times, you haven't given into that temptation. Bravo. You're a hard-working person. You've got stamina. You're not a quitter. Take a short break but always pick up the brush after a rest, or by the next day.

Can positive self-talk actually be such a powerful force? Absolutely. Psychological research has shown over and over again that positive self-reward strengthens behaviour just as negative talk weakens behaviour. Surely none of us would argue that talk such as 'I can't stand to paint anymore. This job is stupid. It won't look any better even if I finish it. I'm no good at this painting business anyway' does not lead to demoralization. Of course it does. Well, what is all that but self-talk? If it can tear down motivation then why is it so hard to believe positive self-talk can't increase motivation? And remember, the more motivated you are and the harder and longer you work, the better you perform. That changes performance-confidence but not feelings of superiority.

Now, what about penalties? Just as it is important to reward ourselves for a job well done, it is equally important to penalize ourselves for a job poorly done. How else are we expected to improve? If we do not make ourselves uncomfortable with negative results then aren't we rewarding negative results?

Remember always that whatever we do in response to an event either encourages or discourages it. So even if we do nothing in response to an event, even then we are affecting it somehow. Doing nothing about an action can sometimes be taken as approval. For example, if you ignore your child's disorderly bedroom, aren't you giving it your approval? And if you ignore your own negative behaviour, that is the same as approving it.

Therefore, I insist again that unless we make ourselves uncomfortable over our errors we are likely to repeat them. To become more disciplined, and thereby more confident, penalties must be applied which are strong enough to discourage further errors.

If you fail to do your daily exercises, don't ignore the slip, make sure you suffer a bit. Make certain to exercise an extra day that week. If that doesn't cure your procrastination, make things even tougher on yourself. Deny yourself a party you'd planned on attending. Or do a nasty chore, such as washing out your garbage can.

If you don't balance your budget in time and you overdraw your account, penalize yourself by balancing your account without the aid of a calculator. That ordeal should cure the problem.

Did you gorge yourself recently and go beyond your weight limit? Make yourself eat plain foods for a week. Perhaps you could offer to work in the kitchen of the Salvation Army, especially as a dishwasher.

Dr Ellis has offered a classic penalty which can be used to discourage a number of indulgences. He advises his clients to send a large donation to an organization they hate, and include a warm letter of praise for the organization's work.

The greatest beauty secret of them all

Ever since people have had enough leisure to allow them to take good care of themselves they have devoted immense energy to keeping their youth and beauty. A beautiful face is a goal which is pursued by practically every person alive, usually starting during the teenage years. It generally goes without saying that those people who have the most stunning looks or physiques not only feel superior in appearance but may even believe they are also better than others because they are more attractive.

Thank God there are strong exceptions to this observation. Many of us are simply not born with the looks of a movie star and will never have faces or figures that will immediately draw attention to ourselves. If we are worthwhile people because of our physical features we may indeed be self-conscious people for all our lives. But such is obviously not the case. The casual observer of the human scene knows full well that there are people in all walks of life and of all ages who are emotionally healthy but who do not have bodies and faces that could be described as beautiful.

What is it, then, that these people possess that makes us think of them as beautiful people? That dimension which transforms average mortals into attractive and handsome people is often described by others as social confidence and inner peace. This quality of being comfortable with oneself without needing to rely on lipstick, powder or curling iron to make one feel acceptable, has the power to make others see us as handsome and beautiful people. This fascinating human quality, which is not detectable on the surface, nevertheless comes through from deep within and makes us feel so comfortable in the presence of such people that we overlook whatever they normally lack in physical features, and we are powerless to judge them as anything but beautiful.

The most important beauty secret of all is to have that sense of self-acceptance which depends upon nothing. It is always there. It does not increase because of the person doing something remarkable, and it does not decrease because the person has seriously faltered in some way. That hidden beauty secret is not found in a perfume bottle or in an expensive suit. It comes from accepting yourself as you are.

What seems to emanate from such persons is a lack of defensiveness which makes them extremely comfortable to be with. They do not find fault gladly in order to feel superior. They have no need to feel superior. Since they are not self-judging they exude a warmth like a soft bulky sweater which embraces us and keeps out the chill on a winter's day.

The secret of beauty is to develop that inner sense of peace that comes from non-judgment. It does not change because of age. It does not change because of good or poor fortune. It is always present, radiating a quiet resignation to the person's human limitations. It accepts one's humanity as being fragile and limited. Therefore, it strives to be the best it can be without neurotically demanding more than it can give. That is the beauty that never dies. Therefore, if you want true and lasting beauty, learn to feel secure and comfortable with yourself. People love that and they will love you for it.

Confidence and risk-taking

Of all the qualities necessary to develop confidence, risk-taking ranks right up there near the top – if not at the top. Without it, confidence-building is not possible. Nor are a great many other wonderful achievements or pleasures.

Take the case of businessmen who start off on a shoestring and a prayer, invest their savings in an idea and end up as millionaires. Ask them how they got rich and they'll always include 'guts' as one of the main qualities all entrepreneurs must possess.

The men who started the movie industry were thought to be fools. So were the men who built the automobile industry. And what about Kentucky Fried Chicken? Colonel Sanders used his retirement income to start his company. The stories of McDonald's, Happy Joe's, Domino Pizza, and Benetton, and those of thousands of companies all over the world, are all similar: someone had an idea, put his or her savings at risk, worked hard and it paid off.

Another example of risk-taking involves the fear people have of aspiring to be their best. Instead, they often aim low and feel safe, only to wish later that they had been more daring. I'm referring to career choices.

It has been my sad experience to counsel a number of intelligent and talented people who stopped their careers at the beginning. Many had the opportunity and ability to enter college and achieve a professional career, but because they doubted their ability to succeed, they avoided the risks of college or graduate school. Some, after working for years in a lesser position, realized gradually that they could have achieved higher.

I have known mature men and women who eventually returned to school to become lawyers or physicians. I have also known middle-management people who saw the light and returned to business school after many years of frustration in a field beneath their true abilities.

Like others who had great business ideas but were afraid to act on them, these people had high career aspirations but wouldn't risk poor grades and flunking out of school to find out just how high they could achieve.

Nurses are another example of low risk-taking. Women are every bit as capable as men of being physicians. Until this past decade we have seen pathetically few of them aspire to an MD degree. In the Soviet Union a far higher proportion of physicians are women than anywhere in the West. Until women take risks and stop settling for less demanding careers, they will not fulfil the great promise they are capable of.

A final example of low risk-taking involves men and women who are pathetically lonely because they won't stick their necks out to risk rejection and make a phone call for a date. Some go to dances and will never cross the room to ask a lady for the next dance. Others would rather stay home evening after lonely evening and never invite friends over for a small party. And all of this just to avoid that supposedly horrible and unendurable pain that comes from being rejected.

How sad! These good people who hurt so much never seem to understand that they repeatedly make two serious errors in judgment: that they will be uncomfortable if they break through their shells and gain a few close friends; and that they will be uncomfortable if they don't. Pain is the price they pay for either decision. Unfortunately, they just don't appeciate the fact that taking risks involves less pain in the long run. Two sayings typify this sentiment: 'The coward dies a thousand times' and 'Faint heart never won fair maid'.

The price

How much effort does it take to improve your skills to the

point where you feel very confident? Do we develop mastery of a sport or of a vocation by performing those tasks one or several hours a day? How hard does one need to work in order to get top grades in order to get into an outstanding university? How many hours should one put into practising piano or some other instrument in order to become professional? How much time and how often should one exercise in order to achieve reasonable physical fitness?

In my experience I find that people vastly underestimate the time it takes to develop a skill to the point where one becomes master of that skill. The typical high-school student is, in my opinion, a sad example of how little some people appreciate the amount of effort it takes to become good at something. High-school children often feel they are able to learn languages, study physics and mathematics, and so forth, and not do regular homework. They count on doing their assignments in study halls or perhaps with an additional half hour at home in the evening. Many will not review course material before an examination but will rely upon their memories instead.

I have on numerous occasions told my clients that if they didn't want to fail a class they would have to do two to four hours of homework a night. Saying that to some high-school students is like hitting them over the head with a sledge hammer. They think everything in life should come easily.

This is something of which foreign students seem to have a better grasp. Oriental students newly immigrated to the United States are achieving academically in remarkable ways. Some are winning spelling contests. Others are getting scholarships in medicine, physics, and mathematics to our graduate schools. Many of them are showing unusual mastery of musical instruments such as the violin, cello or piano. In short, they are quickly making progress which would have been unthinkable for immigrants. Not only must they adapt themselves to a very strange culture and learn a new language, but they outperform American citizens in their own schools. They are clearly not afraid of self-discipline. Their parents are so grateful for being in a country that provides them with wonderful career opportunities that they instil the notion into the minds of their children that practically anything is possible in the United States if they work hard enough.

Moderate performance-discipline was a reasonable attitude to take during those years when we in the United States led the world and had no competition. Now, however, that the Germans and the Japanese are outperforming us in technology, we will have to develop degrees of performance-discipline to which we have never had to aspire before. To do otherwise will eventually weaken our career-confidence while strengthening it for the newcomers.

Japan, for example, teaches its students to strive for the very best and encourages them to do four hours of homework a night. But this goes on six nights a week. These students sometimes attend school six or six and a half days a week, ten months a year.

A word of caution. Hard work can be overdone. To kill oneself in the pursuit of excellence is not much of a reward. I recommend hard work to the point where it would keep us competitive without also creating serious emotional problems.

5

The Third Step:
Make People Respect You

When we analyse the kinds of emotional problems people have, we find that it is the *interpersonal* relationships which give them the most trouble. And among these problems, excessive passivity is one of the worst. So it is extremely important to avoid being dominated by others to an unreasonable degree. Assertiveness training takes on enormous importance, therefore, if one is to be a reasonably happy individual and especially if one wants to be emotionally untroubled. Without assertiveness skills it is almost impossible to have healthy feelings of self-acceptance. So in this chapter, I will be going into the assertiveness process in great detail as I have found it works with my clients and also with me personally.

This process is based on cognitive-behavioural principles, with emphasis on rational-emotive therapy (RET) and the principles of operant conditioning as taught by the famous psychologist, the late Dr B. F. Skinner. This system will teach you to question some of your most cherished beliefs and you will, therefore, probably find them uncomfortable. But do not be discouraged. Read through this entire chapter, not once, but several times, before rejecting my views. And, of course, put my ideas to the test. Start off gradually and learn to assert yourself over little issues. Later, you will deal with those that are most troublesome in your life. If you do, I believe you will do yourself *and* others an immense service.

Examples of passivity

In searching my memory for examples of excessive passivity a number of individuals come to mind. Some of them are adults, some children, and some are males. The overwhelming number, however, are adult females. This is undoubtedly the result of the fact that women are physically weaker than men and are often financially dependent upon them. In addition, women are taught by their mothers and grandmothers that giving in to their husbands is the ideal way to achieve happiness in marriage. They are portrayed as the peace-makers. It has usually been the sons in the family who have been encouraged to pursue education while women have been denied these opportunities. This has left females powerless. And lastly, when a woman becomes a mother and stays home to care for her children she is completely dependent upon the labour of her man. A man in this position might sometimes feel he can safely take liberties with his marriage. If his wife dares to rock the boat she knows she could be without that vital financial support which the man provides. So she adopts the passive strategy in hopes that her being agreeable will make the marriage run more smoothly and give her the security that she and her children need.

These factors, in various combinations, have made some of my clients so dependent and passive that they have permitted infidelity, sexual abuse of the children or physical abuse of themselves. One woman who was trying to gain some control over her adolescent son was repeatedly undermined by her husband, who disagreed with her in front of the boy and made a pal out of him. She was depressed, angry and hurt but did not make too big an issue of this even though she knew the boy was becoming disrespectful of her by disobeying her orders and even calling her vulgar names, while the husband more or less looked on.

I counselled her for less than half a dozen sessions, after which she terminated. It was apparent to me and to her that, under the circumstances, since her husband would not enter therapy, she would have to tolerate the situation rather than endure all the possible consequences that her resisting the boy and the husband would create. That scenario is as old as civilization.

Another woman had been dominated and abused by her father. Later, when she had a family of her own, although she had a very gentle man for a husband, she was still such a passive person that when she worked in an office she soon found herself playing the very passive role she had always played as an adolescent. When asked to answer the telephone at another desk for a co-worker who might be leaving the room, she agreed to do so. In time other requests were made of her: to do extra work, to come early or to stay late, and she always complied. Soon she was skipping her morning and afternoon breaks, and not leaving the office for lunch. When she brought this matter to her superior she apparently protested in such a gentle way that he never saw the seriousness of the situation and did very little to correct it. Over a period of months she became depressed, developed stomach pains, head pains, and a strong dislike for work. Still she performed her duties as best she could, tried to juggle all the balls thrown to her, and felt powerless.

Then she entered counselling. With much explanation and urging I instructed her to change the situation in the office. I helped her see how the problem developed in the first place, and what she could expect from her co-workers when she began to resist their demands.

I was definitely pleased with the progress she made because she slowly but surely overcame her timidity, asserted herself in the workplace in ways which I will describe later in this chapter, and got the respect from the office she had never had before. This had an additional pay-off with her mother-in-law and other relatives with whom she also had been passive. There were often bad feelings generated within the family structure, just as there were in the workplace, but she now understood what would happen if she did not take a stand and she was prepared. Over a period of about a dozen sessions she made substantial changes in her life both at work and at home and ceased being the angelic and yielding woman she had been all her life.

Another woman comes to mind who devoted all her energies to her husband. They had married young, and he now began a series of liaisons with other women, perhaps because he felt he had somehow 'missed out'. Because she was very dependent upon him, she wept, shouted in protest, and moved him out of the bedroom, all to no avail. He correctly sensed that she would not leave him and he could have his way if he just didn't push too hard and force her to divorce him.

To avoid that eventuality he always gave in just enough to quieten her, and when she felt less threatened he would be off on his excursions again, doing as he liked. It was her practice to give him another chance, to believe each of his promises, only to be discouraged again after a period of time when he would break his promises, give her numerous explanations, promise not to do as he had done, and then repeat the whole cycle.

She never seemed to learn that talking was seldom effective with him. Without her realizing it she was rewarding his behaviour, and was utterly baffled by the fact that all her efforts never seemed to have any effect upon him. I showed her over and over why she was unsuccessful and that she would have to take certain risks, but she never managed to do this. Eventually she left therapy and went back to him. I lost track of her at that point. It would not surprise me if she has gone through this cycle a few more times. Perhaps some day she will put an end to this relationship and leave the man, or finally make him so regretful over his unfair treatment that he actually makes a change.

I remember the case of a middle-aged male and the difficulty he had in asserting himself over his rebellious adolescent son. This boy was about sixteen, headstrong, and beginning to experiment with his power. One day, when he was ordered by his father to do a chore, he refused and walked out of the house. The father was too afraid and unsure of himself to meet the challenge and dominate the boy. That was the beginning of the end of his control over his son. From that time on the boy refused to do his chores, refused to practise his musical instrument, and refused to do his homework. He began to get poor grades and eventually quit school.

However, his tendency to indulge himself, something he could now do at will, overflowed into his social relationships. He practised at school and on the playground all the self-centred behaviours he could get away with at home. But there he found things quite different. When he didn't get his way with his playmates and his girlfriends he would act indignant, angry, and behave in such a negative way that he was repeatedly rejected.

When I saw him he was about twenty-four years old. He realized what had happened to him and was now disappointed and angry that his father was so passive when he was growing up and let him get away with such unbelievably permissive behaviour. And it was he who said that he wished his father had been stronger with him and not let him get away with his irresponsible and rude behaviour. He understood quite clearly that he developed a number of bad habits as a result of his father's excessive passivity and which would have been impossible had the adult man stood up to his adolescent son.

This is one of those many cases where children realize that they were taught a number of bad habits by their parents and that they, the children, are not fully responsible for them. They can understand that. What bothers them, however, is the fact that *they* must now go through all the hard work which is required to change those bad habits. Their parents, who are either no longer living with them or who are deceased, cannot make these changes for them.

The signs of excessive passivity

How do you know when you are being excessively passive? The first clue, of course, is when you realize that you are being dominated. When you are repeatedly and continually following the dictates or wishes of other people and somehow seldom getting your own deep desires and needs satisfied, that is the clearest indication that you are being too easy-going and are trying too hard to please others, probably at the cost of getting their approval and love.

Being under the control of other people is a very uncomfortable feeling. Practically every adolescent knows what I am talking about because he or she, in order to grow up, has to confront that issue with parents. There comes a time in the life of every youngster when some confrontation must be attempted in order to make the parents back off and let the child think for himself. People do not want total safety in this world, they want challenge and they are willing to suffer mistakes as long as they know they are the ones who took the risk. And in truth it is *sometimes* better to do your own thing, even against the advice of your elders, because you are not convinced they are right. When you defy authority you may very well find out how foolish you were. But that is an experience a lot of people need in order to get them to change. But since they have made the mistakes on their own, and they are suffering for the mistakes all by themselves, they are usually more easily convinced that they were wrong and have learned something.

To follow every sound piece of advice offered to them denies them that choice of making a mistake and the thrill of making decisions, even bad decisions. It is for this reason that I usually encourage parents to let children alone when they have decided that they must do their thing. Let them suffer the consequences. If a young man does not want to study but chooses to repeat a course in school, then so be it. Dominating him to the point where he rebels gets us to that same point in any event. So why not back off? Let him make his mistakes and learn the hard way. Some of the most important lessons we have all learned have come from the school of hard knocks.

If a person is about to embark on a course which is clearly dangerous or extremely unwise in some other respect then I think his parents need to intervene more vigorously to try and persuade him not to proceed. Marrying too young is one example.

We often do not succeed in dissuading young people from ignoring education, early marriages, and other pursuits. However, when drugs, suicide or other dangerous consequences might follow, then, of course, we need to attempt to dominate them, even against their wishes, and hospitalize them if necessary.

Leaving these exceptions aside, the point is still a valid one that most people do not enjoy domination and that they are usually wise to fight against the loss of control of their lives when the consequences are not fatal.

Those who suffer from excessive passivity invariably feel depressed, inferior and guilty because of the directions their lives are taking without their permission. They simply do not know how not to blame themselves for the loss of control they are experiencing and they then make their problems infinitely worse with their depressions. Once they regain control over their lives their depressions seem to lift noticeably.

Another consequence of excessive passivity is that it weakens the ties that we have with those people who do the dominating. When individuals are controlled by others stronger than they, the latter may enjoy that domination but they dislike and think less of those whom they dominate. We simply don't admire people who permit themselves to be enslaved. This means that a woman who controls her husband loses respect and love for him. Children as well lose the respect for weak parents and will abuse them when they grow up and can stand up for themselves. Adolescent boys are particularly notorious for rebelling against passive mothers. But this can happen at times with passive fathers as well. I well recall a case of a young boy who had a very passive father and the boy found out in short order that he could do as he pleased and not expect any resistance from his father. The mother lost respect for her husband because she could not count on him to keep the boy in line. When the attempt was once made to get the parents to assert themselves against the young man he proceeded to break furniture, throw things around the house, and make a very ugly scene. This was enough to get mother and father to back off and thus give him the rule of the roost. Needless to say, he continued that reign of terror until he left for the army.

This degree of passivity almost invariably has that kind of negative effect on children. They learn great respect for aggression and do not hesitate to use it in dealing with further frustrations in their lives, at least with their families. And why shouldn't they? If they get away with abusive behaviour then that's the same as being rewarded for abusive behaviour. Whatever you are rewarded for you tend to repeat over and over until it no longer brings rewards.

Why people treat us the way they do

If you feel badly about yourself and have wondered most of your life why others don't respect you, you will be most interested in learning why you are repeatedly treated in such an unkindly fashion. Among the more important observations I want you to remember from this book are the two which I will give you in a moment. Read them over and over and memorize them. And the next time you find yourself taken advantage of, immediately call to mind the two pieces of advice which I am about to give you. It will help you explain why these unkind acts are happening to you and will explain in a general way what you need to do in order to prevent that sort of thing from happening in the future.

Principle no. 1: We get the behaviour we tolerate.

Principle no. 2: If you want others to change, you have to change your behaviour first. Which behaviour? Your excessive tolerance.

Let us study this in more detail. The principles of conditioning, as studied by Dr B. F. Skinner at Harvard University, say that when behaviour is reinforced or rewarded it tends to become strengthened. This is the same principle that we use in training seals to juggle balls or dogs to chase sticks.

The clothes we choose to wear, the ideas we believe, the food we eat, and other activities we follow are all the result of the conditioning process. We do what we do because we were rewarded in some manner, great or small, for doing it. If you want to know why somebody is cruel, nasty and abusive you can be fairly sure that that person observed such behaviour when he was growing up. If a boy sees his angry father get his way when he is abusive, he may try the same at school, and will find that he, too, can get what he wants by bullying people. He will be rewarded for these behaviours. When you reinforce an act, it gets stronger.

It does not take a great stretch of the imagination now to ask ourselves why people treat us the way they do. If a behaviour occurs several times we must assume that it was rewarded. When we apply this to ourselves we have to appreciate the fact that if other people are not listening to us very much it is because we have taught them not to do so. If people make promises to us and don't keep them, and this has happened more than twice, we can be sure that somehow the breaking of promises has been rewarded by us. *We get the behaviour we tolerate.*

To turn the perspective around a bit, we might ask ourselves how we have been treating our loved ones, what we have been teaching them about life and whether we have been educating them properly. All we need to do to answer that question is simply to ask ourselves how they are treating us. That tells us what *we* taught them. If our partners are mean to us we have to assume some *indirect* responsibility for that behaviour because it is something we have put up with. Whatever we put up with we're likely to get more of. This principle explains why people who are trying to get along with each other don't – for example, where one partner is a spendthrift while the other picks up the bills. This observation also explains why children won't listen to mother but always listen to father because he gets tough. And if your sex life is not very good, it is in part because you have put up with bad love-making.

A woman asked me at one of my seminars why her son always asked her to wash and iron his shirts on Sunday evening when she was ready to go to bed. I inquired of her as to what she did when he made that request and she said she would do as he asked but also complained that she wished he would remind her earlier in the day so that she could go to bed on time. And every so often on a Sunday evening he would again come to her and ask that she do his shirts late Sunday night. She raised a good question when she asked why he was doing this. After all, she had scolded him for it and registered her complaint, and wasn't that sufficient to teach him not to do it again? I pointed out to her that the boy treated her in this inconsiderate manner because she rewarded him when he did so. He always got the shirts washed and ironed before she went to bed. Even though she protested verbally she nevertheless gave him the clean shirts. I asked her why she simply didn't let the young man go to school without those clean shirts. She replied that she didn't want him to be embarrassed and she didn't want people to think that she was an inconsiderate mother. In other words, she was not willing to pay the price to change his behaviour.

This is an extremely important insight for you very passive people. The chances are that you have a number of people in your life who don't respect you, take advantage of you, and treat you shabbily. Principle no. 1 should make it abundantly clear to you that these people are doing what you have allowed them to do, what you have educated them to do, and what you have rewarded them for doing. Why do people treat you like second-class citizens? Because you reward undesirable behaviour, whether you know it or not.

The second principle of human interaction states that we must change ourselves first before we can get others to change. The moment we decide to alter *our* behaviours, they have to come up with new responses. Therefore, don't look to others if you don't like the way they are, put the responsibility for their treatment of you where it belongs, with you. *You* do something differently and they'll do something differently.

But what do we do? How do we go about altering the behaviours of others whom we have either met briefly or whom we have conditioned and programmed to take advantage of us over a period of months or years?

The assertiveness process

There are three rules to follow if you want to get people to give you co-operation, respect and love.

Rule no. 1: When people treat you nicely, treat them nicely also.

This is not easy to do. Many people have a very difficult time praising others for their fine actions. Parents find it easy to criticize children but difficult to praise them. People are doing positive things for us much more often than they are doing negative things. Yet we have a tendency to focus on faults and mistakes rather than on accomplishments and decent actions.

If others had used Rule no. 1 with you from birth, you would not have inferiority problems today. Your good behaviour would have been reinforced, you would have felt good about yourself, confident about the world, and there would have been little for you to hate. Therefore, I want you to make it a practice to reward others when they have been good to you, and to reward yourself when you have done good things for yourself. Let us make it a habit to reward good behaviour from everyone.

Rule no. 2: If people do something bad to you, and don't realize they are behaving badly, reason with them. But only do so twice.

In more detail, this rule suggests that you turn the other cheek, go the extra mile, show forgiveness, and become completely tolerant in the conviction that those people who have done something bad to you have done it because they are deficient, ignorant or disturbed. There is no reason to be hostile. Assume this is an act you can reason about, and explain in some in detail why it is unacceptable and what you want of these people in the future. Bear in mind, however, that Rule no. 2 applies only when you believe that those people who have acted unkindly really don't know that their behaviour was inappropriate or unkind. If they know that stealing is wrong, or that yelling viciously at a child is dangerous, or that being unfaithful is immoral, then why use Rule no. 2 at all? You don't want to waste time telling people something they already know. When we repeat ourselves and tell them what they are doing wrong, we are simply encouraging them to do the same wrong thing. That applies to two types of people: the immature, and the emotionally troubled. People in those two categories simply do not learn well by reasoning. The fact that they get away with their negative behaviour and get only a lecture instead is reward enough to encourage them to do the very thing they are scolded for. Therefore, *the more you lecture these people the more you train them to do the thing you are lecturing against.*

There are many well-meaning individuals who believe that one should always turn the other cheek and always go the extra mile in the belief that if we continually return positive behaviour for negative behaviour, people will eventually change and develop for the better. I wish this were true. But evidence from psychological research and from everyday experience simply doesn't support it.

If there is one strategy which I think causes more inefficient childrearing and more inefficient handling of conflicts between people it is the overuse of Rule no. 2. We talk too much, we turn the other cheek too much, we unwittingly teach people and program them to do the very things we protest, and then we are amazed that somehow we are not getting anywhere. My recommendation is to give people the benefit of the doubt twice if you're sure that they were truly ignorant of how bad their behaviour was. We owe them that much. But after that, stop the talking, stop the reasoning, stop trying to find out why they do this or why they do that. Stop trying to figure out what it is about them that is making them do this or that. Simply stop all discussion and move on to Rule no. 3.

Rule no. 3: If people do something bad to you and talking to them has not helped, do something equally annoying or discomforting to them, but do it without anger, guilt, other pity, fear of rejection, fear of physical harm, or fear of financial harm.

I know this probably sounds like an unfeeling and very aggressive thing to suggest, but stop and think what choices you have if you are dealing with people you tried to reason with and they have not responded. If people will not listen to reason then isn't it true that either you have to leave them alone and step out of the situation, or increase whatever pressures you have applied to make them more willing to negotiate? When words fail, therefore, actions must take their place. But why actions? What is so sacred about an action that makes it so superior to words? The answer is quite simple. Words actually don't hurt. We can let them hurt if we want, too, but even if we do let them hurt, they are not nearly as bad as the kinds of discomfort and pain we can get from uncomfortable actions.

To be fired from a job is a great deal more serious than being scolded. To be told that you are not loved by your partner is not nearly as painful as being divorced. To be called lazy by your mother because you did not clean up your room is hardly as uncomfortable as it is when she stuffs your things in a garbage bag and throws them out in the garbage. In short, actions speak louder than words. Never was there a folk saying truer than this.

Rules nos 1 and 3 come from the writings of two psychologists, George and Charles Madsen. They have expressed in very simple but powerful language what psychological research established years ago. And that is, that how we respond to situations determines what we will be dealing with in the future. To ignore unfavourable actions is the same as to reward them. If we penalize negative behaviours we will discourage them. Doing nothing about an action does not leave it unaffected. Behaviour is either encouraged or discouraged. It is, therefore, extremely important to stress: if we want good actions to be repeated and negative actions to be diminished, we had better do something about it since to do nothing rewards the behaviour. I believe it was Abraham Lincoln who said: 'Silence is consent'. Therefore, if people step on your toes and you say nothing about it, they are given the impression that stepping on your toes is an acceptable act.

Generally it is advisable to do something fairly similar and sometimes even identical to what others have done to you if you want to give them the message that they have been thoughtless to you and that they had better stop being so. Therefore, if somebody is habitually late in keeping appointments with you, you might try doing the same to him. If a person you loaned money to does not repay the loan on time then do not loan that person money again either for ever, or at least not for a long time. If an adolescent loses his temper at home and breaks things, make the child clean up the mess and pay for the damages.

If your mate promises to be home for a six o'clock dinner and you have gone to reasonable efforts to provide a fine meal and he does not show up or does not call, then eat by yourself and throw the rest of the food away. Do not save it for later so that it can be heated at his convenience.

If one of your children has been impossible, disrespectful, lazy, a law-breaker, and a spendthrift, and you have a ton of money you could leave him, don't do so. Give the money to someone who deserves it.

If your partner drinks too much at a party and you have complained about it twice, simply leave early and without him or her.

If you are talking to someone who is yelling at you over the telephone, and you have tried to be reasonable with that person, hang up.

If your employee has been habitually late, suspend him for a short period of time.

If a relative tries to tell you how to fix up your house, or raise your children, and becomes quite forceful in the process, simply don't have that person over to the house again for a good long time.

Do you begin to get the idea? Thoughtless behaviour does not need to be tolerated and the sooner you protest the sooner it diminishes. But apart from that, your contentment with yourself grows like a corn stalk. Do not lose sight of why we are going through this assertiveness process: primarily, so that we can live more comfortably with others and with ourselves.

The six conditions

Notice that under Rule no. 3 I have listed six conditions that must be observed if you are to become an assertive person. It is not possible to stand up for your rights in an efficient manner if you do not observe each of these six conditions. They are:

Condition no. 1: Avoid anger

It is imperative that you learn to overcome your anger when you are trying to assert yourself. People are more inclined to give in to you if you are doing it in a diplomatic manner. But the opposite also applies: the nastier you are while trying to change other people's negative behaviour, the harder it is to agree with you. Remember we are trying to get cooperation, not war, but when you get angry with others you give them every legitimate reason in the world to strike back.

Some relationships are simply impossible if this observation is not considered carefully. Marriages, in particular, can only work well when people use Rule no. 3 without anger. That happens, incidentally, to be the definition of assertiveness. Assertiveness is when you stand up for your rights *without* anger. Aggressiveness is when you stand up for your rights *with* anger.

I always advocate and applaud assertiveness and I always discourage aggressiveness unless it is a question of self-defence. If someone is out to hurt you seriously and physically then I suggest that you forget all about the niceties of assertiveness and fight for your very life. However, anything short of that is better handled if it is done in an assertive, firm and unangry manner.

When I recommend that we use Rule no. 3 I am not talking about revenge or retaliation, as I shall explain later. I am talking about correction. It is therefore terribly important to remember these observations which will help you remain calm:

1. *You* make *yourself* angry, nobody does this to you.

2. Anger is the result of our making demands out of our wishes.

3. If you never want to get angry again, never make another demand.

4. We make things a great deal worse when we get angry by believing that the people who are frustrating us are horrible and evil because they are not giving us what we think we need.

5. The worst way to make people cooperative is to be very severe with them, beat them, or scream at them.

6. Every time you are angry you are acting like a child who thinks he must have everything he wants.

7. If others are treating you unfairly and frustrating you in serious ways, what do you gain by becoming angry on top of that? Aren't you suffering enough?

Condition no. 2: Avoid guilt

I have already described the dynamics of guilt in Chapter 2, but let me now briefly summarize the major points.

You must do two things in order to feel guilty. First, you must have done something which in your opinion is bad, wrong, immoral, or mean. Second, you must disapprove of yourself because of it.

Doing bad things does not have to make you feel guilty. All of us have made millions of mistakes in our lives and we have hardly felt guilty about the vast majority of them. It's only when we prejudicially pick out certain behaviours which we think are especially bad that we then think we are truly bad and unforgivable because of those particular acts.

My recommendation is never to feel guilty over anything. This means you can choose never to hate yourself for whatever mistakes you have made. Instead, let me ask you to focus on those things which you feel you have done wrongly, to be calm about them (or at least as calm as you can be), not to hate yourself, but to start focusing very intently on what it was that you did incorrectly and to see if you can correct it. By not getting depressed, feeling guilty, or feeling inferior, you are much more likely to focus on your mistakes and correct them than you are if you feel guilty. Feeling guilty usually leads you into punishing yourself for your sins and that does not generally correct the problem for which you are blaming yourself.

Always remember to make a clear distinction between *being* guilty and *feeling* guilty. When we think we *are* guilty, we acknowledge the fact that we have made a mistake or acted badly. *Feeling* guilty means that we now think we are worthless, evil and undesirable people because we have behaved badly. The first is often true. The second is never true, unless you brainwash yourself into thinking it is.

Condition no. 3: Avoid other-pity

If you want to be an assertive person and get tough with people in order to change them for the better, but you then feel sorry for the inconvenience you put them through, obviously your assertiveness is going to come to a screeching halt. How can you make people uncomfortable if everytime you do so your heart melts?

To stop this nonsense it is imperative that you overcome the irrational idea in your head that other people's problems and disturbances should upset and disturb you. Unless you firmly challenge that idea you're not about to become an assertive person and prevent people from taking advantage of you.

Briefly, to overcome that irrational idea it is crucial to realize that caring for people is one thing, but overcaring is another. When our hearts break over the discomfort we give others we really aren't doing them much good. We have to learn to be firm to people *for their own good*. Who wants a surgeon who feels so sorry for the misery he's about to put you through when he cuts out a tumour from your body? Such a person is of no value to you whatever.

A middle-aged male told me that he turned his son over to the authorities because the boy was on drugs. No sooner had he done this than he felt intensely guilty when he saw the police take him off to the hospital. He forgot what he was doing. He forgot that being firm with people is a good thing and that discouraging them from bad behaviour takes courage and is something that we should applaud. He, however, felt he was an evil father and he was depressed over the difficulty he was putting his son through. However, putting his son into a psychiatric ward and making the young man uncomfortable was precisely what was good for him. To weaken at the moment that the father had finally done the correct thing is almost a joke. But people do this all the time. Just as they are finally about to succeed and get some sensible results in their dealings with others, their hearts break, they become emotional mush, and then they back off and reward their children or their spouses for precisely the behaviour they were trying to control. I think this is regrettable and I argue strenuously against it. Other-pity has got to go. *Over-caring* has got to go. But caring for people has got to stay.

Condition no. 4: Do not fear rejection

It is practically impossible to be firm and stand up to others if you fear rejection. This is an enormously important and very powerful fear which makes cowards of us despite our best intentions. As I have already written in my book *Overcoming Worry and Fear* (published in the UK by Sheldon as *Why be Afraid?*) among the greatest fears people have is the fear of rejection.

Those of you who judge yourselves, your worthwhileness, your self-esteem and self-image on the basis of who loves you and who doesn't are bound to run into serious difficulties when you want to stand up for yourselves. Stop and think for a moment what it means to stand up for yourself. It means that you are going to confront someone who is frustrating you. And the person who is frustrating you is often someone who is important in your life. Therefore, if you want to stand up to people you will have to encounter the possibility of their disliking you.

When you are beyond the age of an adolescent you no longer need the approval of your mother and father, of your grandparents, of your husband or wife, of your friends, or your fellow-workers. In short, you do not *need* the approval of anyone in order to be an acceptable human being. You will, of course, suffer certain disadvantages because you are not in good favour with others. But that hardly means that you are somehow less desirable. And that is the main point that you are so concerned about. If it were not for the huge fear of being thought ill of and being rejected by those people who are important to us, we would simply not care so much whether we were rejected. I don't want to make light of this idea of being rejected by important people in our lives but I don't want to make too much of it either. The difficulty most people run into who find themselves dominated by others and who cannot, therefore, be assertive individuals is the fact that they simply will not risk rejection because they think it hurts. It does not hurt unless we *choose* to hurt ourselves. Does this mean that loving relationships are not important to us? Does this mean that we should simply ignore them and casually walk off in the other direction and whistle merrily in the face of rejection? Of course not. Being rejected by people who are important to us is in fact a very sad event. It is a troublesome and uncomfortable experience, of course. But that is all it is. It is no more heartbreaking than we choose to make it. We all survive rejection if we use our heads. Rejection is uncomfortable, I fully agree. But it is not earth-shattering, horrible, terrible, catastrophic, or the end of the world. Cut it out, ladies and gentlemen, and see things the way they really are.

Condition no. 5: Do not fear physical harm

This is the first of the six conditions which *can* destroy our ability to stand up for ourselves which we are not entirely responsible for. The first four which I have previously mentioned are all due to our mismanaging our feelings and this is no one's responsibility but our own. Physical violence, however, is not something we talk ourselves into, it is something forced upon us. And because it is something which comes from the outside and which we have no direct control over it takes on a dimension of seriousness and realistic danger which the other four do not have.

If you cannot talk the person who is threatening you out of using physical harm as a threat then you have a few options, none of them particularly workable. For example, you might practise strengthening yourself through exercise or weight-lifting so that you can actually become a match for the person who is pushing you around. In the process you might also develop your running speed so that, if someone is out to attack you, you might be able to outdistance him. This is good advice to all schoolchildren who are being pursued by a bully. Standing up against him is futile, but outdistancing him with greater speed might spare you to fight another day.

If you are in a marriage where your life is threatened by a violent partner you may want to turn this person over to the law. Of course, you run the risk of greater anger at your partner's hands when he or she returns home. Unfortunately the police are often not much help in domestic quarrels because they find that wives usually do not pursue these matters and press charges against their abusive husbands. So they quieten the situation down, get back into their patrol cars, and leave the woman to face an enraged husband all by herself.

If you are physically equal to the persons who are giving you trouble, and you have reasoned once and perhaps twice about the unfairness of their behaviour, then my recommendation is to fight back as hard as you can and defend yourself. Don't even worry about losing control over your anger. Who cares whether you are technically acting in a neurotic way (by getting yourself upset) when that may be the way you will save your life.

In the event that you cannot resort to a counter-aggression that could actually stop the abusive behaviour, then use other methods that might strike fear in the heart of the aggressor. For example, women, if they are able, can leave for days or weeks, as often as desired. Abusive husbands are not always the most well-adjusted people in the world by any means and they frequently lean and depend upon their wives or lovers for many other satisfactions. When they sober up or calm down they often regret what they have done and are then quite willing to promise changes in the future. It has been my experience that women who use separation as a tool to strike back at these men return too soon. Men shower them with flowers and candy as well as heart-wrenching apologies, but with no clear evidence that they have changed. Simply promising not to get angry is hardly proof that the anger will cease. Anger is a learned behaviour and it cannot be changed in most instances unless the person has been taught how anger is created and how it is removed. If the man in this situation does not read a book on the subject, or talk to a counsellor on how he makes himself angry, then why should the wife believe he has changed in the slightest?

Those unfortunate individuals who have no money to risk a separation, who have certain obligations or children they need to care for, are simply stuck with a bad situation. If matters get worse they have little choice but to get themselves a separation or divorce or live with someone who will put them up for a time until a more harmonious arrangement can be managed. Often nothing is available to these people except to go home and take more abuse until they either fight back and commit homicide, burn the house down, become mentally disturbed, or until the law comes in and arrests the abuser because of complaints by relatives or neighbours. It is hard to imagine that people in such drastic circumstances cannot get away from physical tyranny. Unfortunately it is a fact of life. The weak, the disadvantaged, the uneducated, or the unemployed find themselves in terrible circumstances from time to time, and there is pitifully little they can do about it except tolerate it.

Our society has not protected these people. There are too many adolescents or wives in prison for defending themselves against the brutal treatment of a father or a husband because it was the only way they could survive. They are then accused of murder when society should have been accused of the crime of neglect.

Condition no 6: Do not fear financial harm

Fear of financial harm and fear of physical harm are the two most realistic fears people have every right to be concerned about. These are not frustrations which people talk themselves into, they are conditions which actually exist in reality.

People who believe that the best things in life are free are dreaming. Unless you live in the South Seas and can reach up and grab a banana whenever you like, you must have money to buy clothes and food. Without these basics you will probably feel a loser (leaving aside the fact that your life may be endangered).

There are some people in the world who can be dirt-poor and think of themselves in noble terms nevertheless. Holy men in all countries have always been able to do so. Money simply isn't that important to them. They live off fruit they pick or buy food with the money they've begged. But if you are not one of these detached and religiously driven persons then money makes a lot of difference to you, especially if you have a family. It is for this reason that people who do not have economic clout are practically always under the domination of people who do. The woman who has no education, has poor work skills, and has several children is the most likely victim of an abusive partner because she may literally find herself on the streets if she antagonizes her spouse too much. Women have learned through the centuries to accept their fate quietly and without complaint, at least overtly. They have suffered in silence, to be sure. But their feelings of inferiority have increased in the process.

It is for this reason that I have often advised my young female clients who are thinking of marriage after high school to forget such plans. Women need to stop relying on others for support and should be able to fall back on a career of their own in the event that their marriages do not work. They can use their training and education to leave a sick marriage and take their children with them. I know this is advice which is sometimes given in vain since the heart speaks louder than the head. Regrettably, seventeen- and eighteen-year-old girls will continue to fall in love early in life and think that marriage is the solution to all their problems.

In summary, it is evident that standing up for your rights in an attempt to make someone uncomfortable enough to change undesirable behaviour is difficult or impossible if any of these six conditions are ignored.

These are the six links in a chain, all of which must be strongly connected if we are to pull ourselves through difficult times. If even one of those links is weak the task of standing up for ourselves stops.

Objections to Rule no 3

Returning negative behaviour with negative behaviour simply strikes such an undesirable chord in many people that they are reluctant to use it. They do this for several reasons.

Objection no 1: We lower ourselves to the undesirable level of the people we are complaining of.

True enough. But stop and think that this is not a choice we happily make. Don't forget that I have advised you always to reason with people once or twice when you feel that their behaviours are undesirable. But if that doesn't bring about a change, and you feel they already know that their behaviours are undesirable, then what is the point of talking further? The solution to the problem is to stop using words as the language of choice and use actions instead. As I said before, actions speak louder than words, and so we must now use some of the same actions which these people respect and listen to. So even though I fully agree with you that it is difficult to reduce yourself to immature behaviours, there seems to me very little choice unless you simply want to tolerate the problem.

Objection no 2: Applying Rule no 3 is nothing more than revenge.

If this were true I would certainly not recommend it. We are not trying to get even, we are not trying to get revenge. We are trying to correct undesirable behaviour by one of the only means left to us. We use tough love not because we hate the people we are frustrating but because we wish them well. We want to educate them, to programme them, to train them to behave differently, not to put them down, or harm them for our own delight, nothing of the sort. *This is a helping and loving act* even though the people at the receiving end may not think so. It may take days, weeks, or sometimes years for them to realize how very loving we have been. The classical case, of course, is when we rear our children with firm measures and penalties, and are appreciated for it years later.

To be tolerant of undesirable behaviour is certainly not a loving act. To be *intolerant* of undesirable behaviour *is* a loving act.

Objection no. 3: Two wrongs don't make a right.

Of course they don't. But we must understand that when we try to change people's self-defeating or negative behaviours into positive ones, even though we frustrate them in the process, we are not doing a negative thing. We are doing this to help them grow and become more mature.

It is not the act itself which is a wrong, it is the intention behind the act. If you dismiss someone from your employment because you know that person really doesn't fit into your organization, that is obviously a helpful and thoughtful act. But to fire him out of revenge, spite, and in order to get even, would be an undesirable and negative act on your part. Then it would be returning one wrong for another. Not otherwise.

Objection no. 4: It's like playing games.

We are not playing games when we return bad behaviour with bad behaviour. Simply because we sometimes reciprocate with one frustrating act for another doesn't make the issue a minor one. If you believe that you are playing games when you are returning bad behaviour for bad behaviour then you are really saying that the whole issue isn't very important. So why do it? Giving others the kinds of actions which force them to change their negative actions is very serious business and it is assumed that you would only want to go through such strain and effort because the problems and frustrations are strong enough to warrant them. If not, then don't play games by any means, simply tolerate the situation without resentment.

When to use Rule no. 3

My clients often ask me how they can know when to stand up to a situation and protest. They worry they might be selfish or inconsiderate and make mountains out of molehills. Yet I reassure them that there is a method they can use which is practically infallible in order to determine whether or not something needs to be made an issue of. And that method is to listen to the signals they receive from their bodies. The body usually tells us all we need to know as to how uncomfortable we are. And if we are so uncomfortable that we are no longer *just reasonably content* it is at that point that we had better do something about it.

The body tells us when we have had enough sleep. We wake up. The body tells us when we are tired and need sleep. The body tells us when to have a drink of water and when to stop drinking. The body tells us when to put up with the noise upstairs in an apartment house or when to complain to a superior over some injustice at work. Listen to your body, it is giving you all the information you need. When you feel you are no longer just reasonably content in your relationships with significant others you had better do something about the situation, otherwise you will develop inferiority feelings, and the following three things will happen.

First, you will become unhappy. If that lasts long enough you may even become disturbed. I have worked with thousands of people who have not listened to the inner voices telling them not to tolerate certain injustices. Some of these people suffered mistreatment for twenty or thirty years and were still tolerating these situations with resentment. When you tolerate situations with resentment (Option no. 4) you are bound to become an unhappy person and more than likely also a disturbed person. As a matter of fact, these are the people who constitute the vast majority of psychologists', psychiatrists' and other counsellors' clients. Teaching people to pay attention to their level of contentment would help everyone's frame of mind and reduce neurotic symptoms enormously. It would keep emotional problems at an acceptable level.

Second, you will fall out of love with those who are frustrating you. It makes no difference what your vows were at the altar or how much you love your partner, your children, or your parents. The results are always the same. If you are frustrated long enough by anyone you eventually begin to lose feelings for that person and the love will begin to die.

Third, you will eventually want to leave those frustrating you. I find that to be a perfectly sensible, healthy and normal reaction to extended frustration. Wouldn't you want to leave a job if it made you feel miserable everyday? Wouldn't you want to leave a marriage (or at least fantasize about leaving it) if it were never reasonably satisfying? Practically everyone who has got a divorce or a separation knows what I am talking about. They know full well that they have probably endured mistreatment at the hands of their partners for so long that they became unhappy and disturbed, gradually began to fall out of love and eventually considered ending the relationship entirely.

The four options

I hope I have not given you the impression that Rule no. 3 is the only action we can take whenever we are frustrated. There are actually four options open to us at all times when confronting any frustration. None of them are very desirable but the first three are preferred over the fourth, which I seldom recommend.

Option no. 1: Toleration without resentment
This strategy calls for lowering your expectations by convincing yourself that the issue at hand is hardly serious. You might decide that your children cleaning up their rooms isn't such a big issue after all, so you ignore it. Or you may talk yourself into believing that not getting a wage increase was sad but certainly not the end of the world.

The moment you decide to tolerate a situation without resenting it you eliminate the problem, save yourself a frustration, and protect your feelings from disturbance. In order to get along with all the people we deal with, Option no. 1 is clearly a frequent choice all of us must make daily throughout our lives.

Option no. 2: Protest

If you don't feel you can tolerate a situation without becoming bitter over it then decide to do something about it. Use Rule no. 3 more vigorously each time you are frustrated by matching your frustrator's efforts with your own. Each time you feel frustrated you will be a little bit more uncomfortable and that's the degree to which you will want to increase the discomfort in the person you are dealing with. This option is aptly called the 'cold war' or the 'strike'.

If you don't want a confrontation (since it will lead to ugly scenes and a great deal of discomfort, and it may not work in the end anyway) then you can always go to the next option.

Option no. 3: Separation or divorce

Practically everybody has this option open to them unless they are extremely dependent, minor children, in prison or crippled. I recommend that married couples who are having difficulty with each other may first want to resort to a separation, but only for one or two days. If that doesn't work perhaps another separation, this time for a week, may be a good idea. After that a longer separation of perhaps three to six months is suggested.

Separations give people the opportunity to realize how serious things are and to see what a divorce is going to be like. It is a rehearsal for a divorce. I have known a number of couples who were very eager for divorce but who changed their minds when they lived apart and on a great deal less income.

Option no. 4: Toleration with resentment

This is the choice most people make. Option no. 4 creates all the symptoms which psychotherapy addresses. It is for this reason that I encourage people not to tolerate things with resentment. Surely they can do better by using one of the other three options because they all, for a majority of the time, lead to some relief. Option no. 4 doesn't lead to relief, it leads to more discomfort. So why use it?

Summary

This chapter has presented the dynamics of the third most important technique you need to practise if you want to become a person with reasonable contentment. Make people respect you. They must eventually learn to have a mild degree of fear of your being able to make them uncomfortable. You don't have to be admired, you don't even have to be appreciated, but you had better get people to understand that if they mistreat you they are going to be made equally uncomfortable by you.

Ironic as it sounds, this is a crucial way in which we get people to cooperate and respect us, and to love us. Isn't it strange that we can get more love when we create mild fear? As I said previously, it is difficult to love people whom we don't respect. And it is equally difficult for others to love us if they don't have some mild fear of us. Look about you and examine your behaviour towards your family, your friends or employees and you will see what I am talking about. Children even love us more when they begin to respect (mildly fear) us and know full well that we will not hesitate to make them uncomfortable if they step out of line. They need this kind of control in order to develop controls of their own. Although they may not appreciate this at the time, when they grow up they certainly will.

In this book I have given you the three crucial techniques you need to develop emotional control. I stoutly maintain that if you *never rate yourself* again, either negatively or positively, you will do yourself the greatest service and will find it impossible to feel unworthy again.

Second, learn to *develop your performance-confidence* by working hard and disciplining yourself so that you are fearless in learning as many tasks as you are interested in. Become accomplished at a great many things and you will not likely develop an inferiority complex.

And finally, by using the thoughts which I have offered in this chapter, you need no longer let the people who are important to you turn your dreams into nightmares. You will correct their habits so that you can continue to care for them, even if you need to get firm. This will bring you respect, often to your amazement. And, just as often you will feel more loved than you believed you'd ever be by *not* being tolerant.

6

What Can You Do?

What is success? What is failure?

As you struggle to achieve a healthy emotional life you will
have many relapses. One day you will rate yourself, you will
procrastinate and you will permit yourself to be manipulated.
The next day you will not rate yourself, you will face difficult
tasks rather than put them off, and you will stand up for your
rights. One day you will think you're succeeding, the next that
you're failing.

That's inaccurate thinking. What I have just described is a
success on both days. Most people don't agree because they
define success only when they are doing well. It does not occur
to them that not doing well is also success. How can this be?
Because we are succeeding always as long as we are learning.
Doing badly is just as valuable an experience for learning as is
doing well.

Doing things correctly tells us what we did right and what
we want to repeat. Doing things incorrectly tells us what we
did wrong and what we want to avoid.

When you begin learning a new task you have little or no
idea of what it takes to master that task. Skiing, baking,
playing the violin, and hundreds of other skills are all
unknown to you until you begin mastering them. At first you
have little idea what works and what doesn't. That's why
mistakes are so important. They teach you what to avoid. Can
you call that failure?

Failure happens only if you do one of two things after you
make mistakes: the first is if you give up trying (for then you
cannot learn what to avoid); the second is if you do not analyse
what you did wrong to make the mistake in the first place.

As long as you are trying, you are succeeding. Granted, at
first you will only succeed at a low level. As you learn what you
are doing incorrectly, you will succeed at higher levels, a little
bit at a time. After much discipline and hard work your

performance will come closer to your potential ability. *That* process is what you should define as success. Your personal success may seem great to you but little to others, but that is not important unless you make your living at that activity. If you are an amateur you need only compete against your personal potential. Aim for complete perfection relative to *your* potential. But if you fall short of that mark, remember, there's nothing wrong with being an amateur pastry chef, or an intermediate skier.

Where do I go from here?

We all want our loved ones to be happy and healthy people. You can help them greatly if you take an active part in helping them not rate themselves, not put off to tomorrow what should be done today, and not let people take advantage of them. When you do that you model the healthiest behaviour your partner or children could learn. The behaviour you teach and the behaviour you practice determine the kind of model you present to your loved ones.

To do this most effectively, follow the recommendations I have made in this book. In short, make sure you don't attack people's egos by rating *them* as bad if they do something bad, or praising *them* if they do something great. If that's hard for you to do, it may be because you have a fear of intimacy or a fear of competition. If you have either or both of these fears it will be very difficult for you to praise the fine things your loved ones do.

If you fear intimacy, you can't tell your partner: 'I love you. I like all the nice things you do for me. Living with you is great. I'm lucky to be married to you.' You can't talk to loved ones if you can't open up and make yourself vulnerable to laughter or rejection.

And God forbid that you are so insecure you can't compliment your spouse or kids because you don't want to be outshone. People like you make it so hard for your loved ones to think about themselves in a healthy way that your families end up more disturbed than they would be if you were not afraid to let others know what kind thoughts you have of them.

Back up words with action. It's not enough to tell your wife you love her, it is very important to demonstrate that with a kiss or an affectionate hug. The expression of love through touch is far more important than many people think. They have probably not been raised by affectionate or demonstrative parents, so they don't know how to give physical love. Instead, they act like emotional robots. No hello kisses. No goodbye kisses. No locked arms when strolling around town. And I shudder to think what sex is like with such cold fish. Worse yet, what is it like to be raised by one or two loving but cold parents?

There are other ways to give your loved ones the strength and security they need to overcome feelings of inferiority. Simply help them out when they are desperate. If you can afford to help them with a car, or a downpayment on a home, or give them furnishings or clothes, why not do so? Everyone needs a helping hand in times of bad luck. Besides, help at the right time reduces stress and helps prevent the development of neurotic patterns; feelings of inferiority especially are less likely.

Knowledge is power. The more you know about human behaviour the more you are likely to be psychologically healthy. Therefore, let me introduce you to some of the books you may find extremely useful as you attempt to achieve self-acceptance.

The New Guide to Rational Living (Prentice-Hall, Englewood Cliffs, NJ, 1961), by Albert Ellis and Robert Harper is an excellent book to acquaint you with the fundamentals of emotional disturbances. This was certainly one of the most important books which started me in using cognitive-behavioural techniques in my private practice.

How to Live with a Neurotic (Crown Publishers, New York, 1957) by Dr Ellis, is another must for anyone living or working with difficult people. It makes a great deal of sense and applies to a wide variety of the difficulties people have with people.

The Institute for Rational-Emotive Therapy at 45 East 65th Street, New York, NY 10021, sells many other books, audiotapes, and videotapes which the layman and professional counsellor can avail themselves of to great advantage, especially books by Windy Dryden, Maxie Maultsby and Ray DiGiuseppe.

A Challenge to Change, by Terry London, is very readable and filled with much stimulating information. This book has just recently been published by Garfield Press of Evanston, IL.

I would also like to recommend several books which I have written and which have proven to be popular with the public. *The Rational Management of Children* (Libra Publishers, San Diego, CA, 1972; in the UK, *How to Bring up your Child Successfully*) was my first published book and has been a favourite with rational-emotive therapists since 1972. It covers the common errors parents make in rearing children and also explains in detail how common emotions such as fear, depression and anger arise in children and how they can be reduced.

Reason in Pastoral Counseling (Westminster Press, Philadelphia, 1972) is currently out of print, but if you search hard for it, there are still copies to be had here or there in the United States. It was written for ministers who are looking for practical and quick ways to give psychological help without violating their religious views.

The following nine books are all in print, published in the US by Westminster/John Knox Press, Louisville, KY, and in the UK by Sheldon Press.

Overcoming Depression (in the UK, *Depression*), *Overcoming Frustration and Anger* (*Calm Down*), *Overcoming Worry and Fear* (*Why be Afraid?*), and *Overcoming Jealousy and Possessiveness* (*Jealousy*) teach you to understand and reduce these painful conditions.

How to Do What You Want to Do teaches you to face tough tasks, to motivate yourself and bring out the potential you have but which often remains untapped.

How to Stand up for Yourself, How to Get the Most Out of Life (in the UK, *How to Be Your Own Best Friend*), and *The Three Faces of Love* (*How to Love and be Loved*) concentrate on developing assertiveness skills. Chapter 5 of this book covers some of the material in these two books.

My thoughts on love and marriage are covered in *Marriage Is a Loving Business* (in the UK, *Making Marriage Work*).

Life is short and we only have just so much time to educate

ourselves. If you waste time reading books which are not helpful, you will do yourself a poor service. At the cost of appearing all-knowing, I will risk your criticism and advise you of the types of books you are better off avoiding.

First, don't bother reading books which teach self-love or self-rating of any kind. I hope I have given you sufficient explanation already why such books would not be helpful.

Second, avoid books which want you to deal primarily with superficial changes rather than deep, philosophical changes. It's fine to be shown how to dress smartly, how to be socially polished, or to be well read so that you can carry on a stimulating and intelligent conversation. However, even though these books may increase performance-confidence, the gains are soon lost when others see below the surface. Not good enough.

For meaningful peace of mind we must alter our irrational thinking habits, not our after-shave lotion. What we *think* about rejection is much more important than what we must do to avoid rejection.

Whether these philosophical issues are expressed in the language of rational-emotive therapy, or in the words of other cognitive-behaviourist schools is not terribly important. What is crucial is that the book you are reading teaches you, at the very least, the following ideas:

1. We upset ourselves, others do not.
2. Rejection does not hurt.
3. Doing badly does not make you a worthless person. Nothing does.
4. It is not catastrophic if things don't go as you'd like.

If you don't come across these ideas, that book better have a lot of other powerful material to make it worth finishing.

Getting maximum value from this book

The books I have recommended form an integral part of the reading I ask my clients to do. It reduces the number of sessions because the client will be learning a great deal of material during the week or two before I see him or her again.

In addition, my clients can study ideas I introduce them to, and they can do it repeatedly and at their leisure. Then, when we meet again, we can go over any issues which are not clear. They often bring the book with them. Almost always I notice that the clients have underlined sentences or ideas which were important to them. I strongly recommend this practice to you. You'll be able to flip through the book and pick out major ideas very easily.

Another way to learn this material – in fact, it is one of the very best – is to teach it to others. You'd be amazed at how it challenges your knowledge of psychology when you try to help others. People will question you the way they question me. And let me tell you how that keeps me on my toes. Try defending yourself sometime when your teenage son or mate tells you you're weird because you believe that doing good doesn't make you good. If you're unsure of your reasoning it will soon show as you try to defend yourself. And, if you can defend yourself it will make you more convinced than ever that you were right.

Giving therapy is the same as receiving therapy. That's what I feel with practically everyone I counsel. We're both learning, but I get it free.

You protest, no doubt, that you are not a psychologist and should not presume to tell others about their dynamics. But why not? When you receive counselling, what do you think is happening to you anyway? Aren't you learning about what causes emotional problems and how to avoid these painful conditions in the future? Of course you are. Well, if you know so much more than others, why not help them with all the interesting things you know? You'd pass on anything you learned in a first-aid class, wouldn't you? Would you not tell your children how to care for their teeth after a dentist instructed you? Surely you wouldn't keep that information to yourself merely because you weren't a dentist, would you?

So get busy. Spread the word. If asked, educate. Don't be shy, use anyone who is interested to give you opportunities to think out loud and thus to improve your health. *The more you teach, the more you learn.* Frankly, that's one reason why I have made my original contributions on the subject of love and marriage, or on assertiveness. Without my clients I'm sure I would never have had the insights which have actually thrilled me.

There you have it. Read this book more than once. You can't possibly absorb it all in one reading. And work on this problem until you learn to go beyond self-esteem and beyond self-love. Instead, strive for self-acceptance.

I wish you the best. Should you want to contact me, write:

Paul A. Hauck, PhD
Suite 302, 1800 3rd Avenue
Rock Island, IL 61201

or call 309-788-6374.